Refining Practices That **BOOST** Student Achievement

ROBERT LYNN CANADY

CAROL E. CANADY

ANNE MEEK

Solution Tree | Press
a division of
Solution Tree

555 North Morton Street
Bloomington, IN 47404
800.733.6786 (toll free) / 812.336.7700
FAX: 812.336.7790

email: info@SolutionTree.com
SolutionTree.com

Visit **go.SolutionTree.com/instruction** to download the free reproducibles in this book.

Printed in the United States of America

Library of Congress Cataloging-in-Publication Data

Names: Canady, Robert Lynn, author. | Canady, Carol E., author. | Meek, Anne,
    author.
Title: Beyond the grade : refining practices that boost student achievement /
    Robert Lynn Canady, Carol E. Canady, and Anne Meek.
Description: Bloomington, IN : Solution Tree Press, [2017] | Includes
    bibliographical references and index.
Identifiers: LCCN 2016051339 | ISBN 9781943874040 (perfect bound)
Subjects: LCSH: Academic achievement. | Achievement motivation. | School
    improvement programs.
Classification: LCC LB1062.6 .C25 2017 | DDC 371.2/07--dc23 LC record available at
    https://lccn.loc.gov/2016051339

Solution Tree
Jeffrey C. Jones, CEO
Edmund M. Ackerman, President

Solution Tree Press
President and Publisher: Douglas M. Rife
Editorial Director: Sarah Payne-Mills
Managing Production Editor: Caroline Weiss
Senior Production Editor: Tonya Maddox Cupp
Senior Editor: Amy Rubenstein
Copy Editor: Ashante K. Thomas
Proofreader: Elisabeth Abrams
Editorial Assistants: Jessi Finn and Kendra Slayton

Acknowledgments

Robert Lynn Canady wishes to acknowledge and thank hundreds of educators, parents, and colleagues who for over forty-five years have listened, commented, critiqued, and encouraged him to continue his work with improving educational opportunities for thousands of students. That work includes crafting creative, data-driven schedules for elementary, middle, and high schools that include (1) academic supports for students during the school day, (2) balanced workloads for both teachers and students, (3) blocks of time that provide opportunities for students to actively engage in learning, and (4) strategies for providing teachers with small instructional groups by employing the principles of parallel block scheduling.

In 1989 he coauthored an article, published in the *Phi Delta Kappan*, titled "It's a good score! Just a bad grade." Based on the reception of that publication and the workshops that followed, he began an examination of the history of grading policies and learned that many such policies have a negative influence on student motivation and achievement. One of the most influential concepts he discovered is that it is important for grading policies to allow students to learn from failure—not just be sorted and graded. In fact, success often depends on a person's being resilient and persistent in analyzing how and why failure occurred and being able to start over. If we want to succeed in increasing the number of college- or career-ready graduates, we must have policies that help students begin again, providing opportunities and supports such as those illustrated in this book.

The authors thank Tonya M. Cupp for her skills in organizing the manuscript and for her editing. It has been a pleasure working with her. We also want to thank and acknowledge the work of Kimalee Dickerson, a second-year PhD student in educational psychology at the University of Virginia, who assisted by researching and editing this book.

Solution Tree Press would like to thank the following reviewers:

Jonathan Cornue
Staff and Curriculum Development
Madison-Oneida Board of Cooperative
    Educational Services
Verona, New York

Kevin Ericson
Special Education Teacher
Nevada High School
Nevada, Iowa

Kendra Hanzlik
Instructional Coach
Prairie Hill Elementary School
Cedar Rapids, Iowa

Jeremy Heeringa
Instructional Coach
Bettendorf Middle School
Bettendorf, Iowa

Michael Huber
Director of Curriculum and
    Professional Development
Portage Public Schools
Portage, Michigan

Benjamin Kitslaar
Assistant Principal
Jackson Elementary School
Elkhorn, Wisconsin

Kirsten Mahoney
Science Department Chair
York Community High School
Elmhurst, Illinois

Andy Pattee
Superintendent
Cedar Falls Community School District
Cedar Falls, Iowa

Tara Reed
Fourth Grade Language Arts and
    Social Studies Teacher
Hawk Elementary School
Corinth, Texas

Kim Timmerman
Principal
Adel DeSoto Minburn Middle School
Adel, Iowa

Maranda Van Cleave
Principal
Greene County Intermediate School
Grand Junction, Iowa

Dave Versteeg
Superintendent
Montezuma Community Schools
Montezuma, Iowa

Matthew Wachel
Assistant Principal
English Landing Elementary School
Prairie Point Elementary School
Kansas City, Missouri

Brad Weston
Principal
Fairdale High School
Fairdale, Kentucky

Visit **go.SolutionTree.com/instruction** to
access materials related to this book.

Table of Contents

Reproducible pages are in italics.

Chapter 3

How Poverty Creates Variables That Affect Achievement

PART II Implement Solutions to the Problems

Chapter 4

Improve Grading Practices and Policies

Chapter 5

Effectively Address Poverty and Its Variables

Chapter 6

Rethink Scheduling

About the Authors

 **Robert Lynn Canady, EdD,** is professor emeritus and former chair in the Education Leadership, Foundations and Policy department at the University of Virginia. He has taught grades 6 through 12 and served as principal of elementary, middle, and junior high schools in Tennessee and Kentucky. He also served as program director of staff desegregation, curriculum, and personnel in central offices in Chattanooga and Oak Ridge, Tennessee. Robert has worked with school districts in forty-six states and with schools in the Virgin Islands and Dependent Schools in Germany. Major presentations have focused primarily on grading practices, active teaching strategies, implementing programs for at-risk students, accelerating literacy achievement for students in the primary grades, and using a variety of scheduling and instructional strategies to restructure schools.

During his teaching career at the University of Virginia, Robert received the Phi Delta Kappa Distinguished Service Award, the Outstanding Professor Award in the School of Education, and two universitywide awards for distinguished teaching and service. In 1997, the Virginia Association of Secondary School Principals presented him the Lamp of Knowledge Award for his contributions to the field of education. The Virginia Association for Supervision and Curriculum Development named him 1998 Educator of the Year. In 2004, the Virginia Association of Elementary School Principals presented him with the Pathfinder Award in recognition of his years of leadership in enhancing the quality of education in elementary and middle schools across the Commonwealth of Virginia.

In addition to publishing numerous articles in educational journals, Robert has served as general coeditor of seven books relative to teaching strategies designed for block schedules, and he has coauthored five books related to school policy and block schedules.

He received his bachelor of science degree from Austin Peay State University, his master of arts degree in curriculum and instruction from Peabody College, Vanderbilt University, and his doctorate in education from the University of Tennessee, where he majored in administration and supervision with collateral studies in educational psychology and industrial and personnel management.

To learn more about Robert's work, visit www.robertlynncanady.com.

 **Carol E. Canady, PhD,** is a literacy consultant, having consulted with school districts in Alabama, Connecticut, North Carolina, Ohio, Tennessee, and Virginia. Her passion is empowering educators with strategies that reduce student failure, primarily by institutionalizing administrative and literacy practices that produce accelerated reading gains. Her consulting focus includes: (1) teaching teachers how to use various assessment measures and instructional strategies within response to intervention; (2) using word study and fluency instruction as bridges to effective reading comprehension; and (3) scheduling and implementing small-group literacy teams to accelerate reading achievement in the early grades.

Carol develops primary-grade curriculum and makes curriculum recommendations aligned with standards with a focus on accelerating reading foundation skills. In her private consulting practice, she provides diagnostic services and then develops and demonstrates how to implement individual lesson plans for students who are reading below grade level to help them progress at an accelerated pace of two to three years in one school year. In schools with an intervention and enrichment period, Carol recommends enrichment units for students who are reading proficiently, with a goal of having those students move to advanced reading and writing levels.

Carol was an assistant professor of early childhood and teacher education at three universities in Ohio. She has also taught undergraduate and graduate courses in literacy assessment and instruction and in children's literature, with a focus on prekindergarten through third grade. Prior to teaching in higher education, Carol was a teacher, counselor, and literacy coach in grades K–8 for thirteen years. As a literacy coach, she pioneered literacy teaming and assisted schools in high-poverty school districts to experience accelerated reading progress.

Carol received her doctorate in reading education from the University of Virginia. She has also published in various educational journals. Her 2012 *Educational Leadership Online* article coauthored with Robert Lynn Canady, "Catching Readers Up Before They Fail," describes strategies for accelerating reading gains to get all students reading on grade level by third grade. She currently serves as an elementary school reading specialist.

To learn more about Carol's work, visit www.CanadyEd.com.

 **Anne Meek, EdD,** taught kindergarten, summer Head Start, and first grade, and then became a Title I reading specialist in Memphis, Shelby County, and Knoxville, Tennessee. In Knox County, Tennessee, she became an elementary principal, then an elementary supervisor, conducting more than one thousand classroom observations and follow-up conferences. She chaired the state curriculum committee to develop the first set of basic skills in reading for the state of Tennessee. She also served as editor of *Tennessee Educational Leadership* for the Tennessee Association for Supervision and Curriculum Development.

Anne then became managing editor for *Educational Leadership* at the Association for Supervision and Curriculum Development (ASCD) in Alexandria, Virginia. In addition to reviewing both solicited and unsolicited manuscripts and then preparing the selected manuscripts for publication, she contributed numerous columns for *Educational Leadership* and authored, acquired, and edited several books, including her own *Designing Places for Learning* and *Communicating With the Public.* She presented sessions at ASCD annual conferences and state and regional meetings throughout the United States. She later served as director of publications for the Developmental Studies Center in Oakland, California. Subsequently, she became an assistant superintendent for the Virginia Beach City Public Schools in Virginia, directing central office communications and providing executive services to the school board and superintendent. Later, she served as senior program specialist for the Education Statistics Services Institute in Washington, DC.

Anne has provided grant writing services for several projects in Virginia, as well as developmental editing services for ASCD books. She served as grant writer and coordinator for the Commonwealth Educational Policy Institute at Virginia

Commonwealth University in Richmond throughout the implementation of *LEADERS Count—In Virginia Schools*, which the Council of Chief State School Officers administers and the Wallace Foundation funds.

Anne received her bachelor of science from the University of Tennessee at Martin, and both her master's degree in elementary education and her doctorate in education in curriculum and instruction from the University of Tennessee, Knoxville.

To book Robert Lynn Canady, Carol E. Canady, or Anne Meek for professional development, contact pd@SolutionTree.com.

I have come to a frightening conclusion. I am the decisive element in the classroom. It is my personal approach that creates the climate. It is my daily mood that makes the weather. As a teacher I possess tremendous power to make a child's life miserable or joyous. I can be a tool of torture or an instrument of inspiration. I can humiliate or humor, hurt or heal. In all situations it is my response that decides whether a crisis will be escalated or de-escalated, and a child humanized or dehumanized.

—Haim G. Ginott

Introduction

Beyond the Grade: Refining Practices That Boost Student Achievement is not just another book about grading. It builds on the urgent need for increased student achievement that promotes college and career readiness, highlighting the need for a major paradigm shift from traditional to innovative thinking. Within this fundamental shift, implementing procedures for constantly assessing student growth, crafting schedules that include daily time for student support, and changing traditional grading practices are critical first steps for making the necessary and significant changes.

The timing is right for examining traditional or long-standing grading practices. Although not all states have adopted the National Governors Association Center for Best Practices (NGA) and the Council of Chief State School Officers' (CCSSO) Common Core State Standards (CCSS), many, like Indiana and South Carolina, have similar versions. In the 21st century, more schools than ever have standards in common. Schools across states can base their grades on similar criteria (Haycock, 2001; NGA & CCSSO, 2009). Now is the time for schools to adopt standards-based grading, which focuses on content mastery instead of hierarchical grades. Common standards facilitate making this change. While moving to standards-based grading, faculty can educate themselves about and advocate for other structural changes that provide the needed support, including alternate schedules and dethroning seat time requirements. In addition, staff can craft schedules that include student support during the school day. We offer scheduling examples to do just that in this book.

Changing schools to the degree we suggest is not easy. Deep-seated cultural beliefs have to be challenged; debates with all stakeholders must be conducted; and practices related to student failure and support need to be re-examined. The journey is not easy, but it is a journey worth taking. It is a journey that our students desperately need and that the world economy needs. We hope many schools will join us in making the journey and that this book answers some of the *why* and *how* questions for those willing to begin the journey.

A Need for Lasting Change

Lasting change in grading practices requires building professional and public support. That support comes through extensive study, data analysis, and debate. *Beyond the Grade* responds to backlash—from colleagues, administrators, politicians, and community members—that may occur when teachers or schools work in isolation to change grading practices. Teachers often have a more important role in struggling students' success than they do with compliant students. Personally motivated to make good grades, compliant students usually accept policies without questioning them and follow the rules. Changing unfair grading practices is more critical for the success of low-achieving students than for those students who succeed in school despite policies and practices. Low-achieving students often face major challenges in their family lives, such as lack of consistent and dependable parental support, limited access to educational resources, and persistent economic instability (Morsy & Rothstein, 2015; Van Horn et al., 2009).

As we know so well, students come to school with many differences—health and growth, talents, experiences, emotional needs, and levels of support from parents and families. We must take such differences into account when working with at-risk students to increase the success of a larger number of students and reduce the number of dropouts. We must use individualized or flexible time lines for them to achieve mastery of material and to help these students meet learning goals. We must make certain that all struggling students within the school have at least one adult they trust and see as their advocate, both in and out of school. That trustworthy adult is the go-to person when a student has questions, dilemmas, problems, and issues. This person can also provide well-informed answers when school-related questions come up in conversations with people in the community. This adult's reward is measured in satisfaction in keeping the student in school, increasing the student's likelihood of getting and keeping a job after graduation, and better preparing the student to provide a positive family life in the future—and sharing correct information with citizens in the community. Struggling students must not see school policies and school personnel as placing roadblocks in their paths to success. Instead, we must institutionalize policies and practices that *insist* students make up all work and that *support* students to do so, even if they have acquired the habit of *not* making up their work (Hill & Nave, 2009). Low-achieving students must learn that when they come to school and work while in school, they will receive payoff for their work.

Before we can successfully implement significant changes in grading practices, it is critical for all stakeholders to study the issues associated with grading practices and to develop a deep understanding of *why* changes are needed.

This Book's Organization and Audience

Beyond the Grade deconstructs traditional teaching and grading practices and presents a better way. We re-examine the very foundations of school—schedules, homework, grading—and present viable alternatives.

This book is presented in two parts. Part I presents the problems; part II presents possible solutions. In part I, chapter 1 lays out the *why now*. Chapter 2 examines grading practices. Chapter 3 discusses how grading issues and student issues abut directly with student achievement.

Once we address the fundamental shift in thought, part II offers strategies for implementing forward-thinking approaches to assessment and grading within real school contexts. Chapter 4 explains the benefits of standards-based grading. Chapter 5 reveals how homework can help instead of hinder achievement. Chapter 6 presents a plethora of schedules, from elementary to high school, including alternative schools, that enable teachers to provide the support students need. Each chapter ends with reflection questions. Visit **go.SolutionTree.com/instruction** to access these free reproducibles.

This book is for educators—administrators and teachers—who are serious about going beyond grades to increasing educational achievement for more students.

Where to Go From Here

Of course, variations in curriculum standards implementation, widespread differences in teachers' experiences, and local community expectations generate differing interpretations and lively discussions of grading practices. In this book, you'll encounter several in-depth examinations of grading practices and principles, discussions and examples of grading policies with varied effects on academic achievement and student success, and descriptions of many factors associated with student achievement and grading practices.

Throughout this book we suggest and describe specific actions that school personnel, with support from multiple stakeholders, can implement to increase the chances that more students will not only graduate from high school but also will be fully prepared to lead financially independent lives. The following lists the major actions educators should do to support such efforts and to attain those goals.

- Implement student grading practices that fairly and honestly indicate what a student has learned and what remains for the student to master.

- Reassess the major purpose of grades. This change, at a minimum, will require schools to separate reporting instruments into nonacademic and academic reports, and the academic reports must focus on mastery of content and skills.

- Increase structural support for students throughout the school day. In the United States, more than 50 percent of our students come from low-income families. Different elementary, middle, and high school schedules can provide student support during the school day as illustrated in chapter 6 (page 71).

- Apply resources to accelerate literacy achievement in the early grades. In the United States, fewer than 40 percent of students leave grade 3 proficient in literacy (National Center for Education Statistics [NCES], 2015a). Visit **go.SolutionTree.com/instruction** for literacy data.

You can see that we have a lot to think about. We will address these issues and many more in the remainder of this book.

Assess Problems With Traditional Grading Practices

PART I

We have reason to implement standards-based grading because it assumes most students, given the right support, can master content. It is time to review grading practices and assessment issues, especially how we calculate and determine grades, and what they communicate to students, parents, and teachers about individual learning and personal effort. Grading issues are not limited to local school districts', states', or provinces' policies and practices. In classrooms, individual teachers may calculate students' grades based on many variables, such as averaging grades earned throughout the grading period, including or excluding homework grades, carrying over grades from the previous grading period, and so on. All these factors are a major source of different interpretations of grades. For example, is it professional and reasonable for one mathematics teacher to count a student's homework as 40 percent of a grade while another mathematics teacher does not consider homework at all in calculating final grades? Should one teacher count a project as 50 percent of a student's final grade while another teacher counts the same project as 20 percent of the final grade?

The variations in grades given by teachers who determine their own measures and values often reflect uneven treatment of students. Such variations in grading primarily affect low-achieving students whose work is inconsistent rather than the high-achieving students who can rely on strong support systems outside of school and, therefore, *consistently* perform well (Morsy & Rothstein, 2015; Van Horn et al., 2009). Therefore, inconsistent grading practices remain a troublesome issue, as 21st century schools are expected to educate a larger, more diverse student population. We'll dive into these issues in the following chapters.

CHAPTER 1

Why It's Time to Reassess

Ranking students based on their grades became a prominent function in public schools not long after compulsory education became mandatory in 1918 (WiseGeek, n.d.). Ranking students by *sorting and selecting* them made sense when jobs were available even for those with very little schooling. As long as the U.S. economy was built on low-skilled labor, sorting and selecting those students who should continue on to the next level, be it grades 6, 9, 12, or college, was an important and expected role of teachers and schools.

But the world is different now. Graduating from high school has become a basic step in finding employment. Our own economic survival may well depend on our performing this function at a higher level than we have in the past. There is ample research that it makes financial sense to significantly improve literacy in grades preK–3 (Allington, 2011; Karoly & Bigelow, 2005); and that improvement is critically important if we expect to reduce the number of students struggling with deficits in literacy and mathematics. Increasing the *achievement* of students living in poverty could be the most cost-effective way to reduce poverty, which in turn could reduce government social services and crime (Gould, Weinberg, & Mustard, 2002). It is cyclical.

Now is the right time to re-examine teaching and grading policies. The job market is different. Education, employment, and poverty are proven to be linked. The grade inflation occurring in many high schools contributes to increased college dropouts (Goodwin, 2011). Standardized assessments make it easier to transition to this change. But first, take a look at how school's purpose has changed over time.

Education, Employment, and Poverty

U.S. schools began using standardized grading systems during the early 20th century. During this time, attendance became legally mandatory, and the number of public high schools grew from five hundred to ten thousand (Lassahn, n.d.). Personalized descriptive student reports became less feasible. Schools began using percentages and letter grades, which introduced many grading debates around criteria variations and grading-scale variations.

With more students entering public schools and the shifting focus on efficiency, grading in essence became a selection tool to determine who would fail and who would progress to the next educational level. The sort-and-select practice was advantageous for a society that required a relatively low- or semi-skilled labor force. Sorting between the labor force and higher education levels became a public school function.

But now it's time to reassess our grading practices. By contrast, public schools of the 21st century do not have the luxury of high failure rates. Because of the outcomes—high failure rates and a glut of uneducated employees in a high-skill market—traditional grading practices are no longer acceptable. Now schools are tasked with making more students college and career ready. Why? Because across all age, sex, and ethnicity categories, students who do not complete high school have a poorer chance of securing employment than those who complete high school or receive a college degree; students, along with the families they create, who never receive a high school diploma that prepares them for a career or college are almost guaranteed a life of poverty (NCES, 2008). Undereducated members of our society often suffer from poverty and many require social and health supports; and if they spend time in the justice system, the personal and societal costs are even greater (Greenberg, Dunleavy, & Kutner, 2007; NCES, 2008). That's why it's not an exaggeration to say that success in school is perhaps the most important factor enabling citizens to lead financially secure lives, unlike in the past. Educators are living and teaching in a time that demands adjustment. See table 1.1.

You can see in table 1.1 that there is a 26 percent difference in the employment rates for ages twenty to twenty-four between students who do not finish high school (51.5 percent) and those who earn a bachelor's degree or higher (77.5 percent). Even completing high school significantly improves students' chances of securing employment, giving them a 16.6 percent advantage over students who do not complete high school.

Table 1.1: Employment Rates Related to Education Levels*

Age	Less Than High School Completion	High School Completion	Bachelor's or Higher Degree
Twenty to twenty-four years old	51.5 percent	68.1 percent	77.5 percent
Twenty-five to sixty-four years old	63.6 percent	76.3 percent	85.7 percent

Expressed as percentages of the U.S. civilian population, excluding military personnel.

Source: NCES, 2008.

Table 1.2 illustrates conditions in earnings and unemployment rates according to levels of educational attainment among those twenty-five and older working full time. A person is defined as unemployed if he or she does "not have a job, [has] actively looked for work in the prior 4 weeks, and [is] currently available for work" (United States Department of Labor, Bureau of Labor Statistics, 2014).

Table 1.2: Earnings and Unemployment Rates by Educational Attainment

Education Attained	Unemployment Rate in 2015 (Percent)	Median Weekly Earnings in 2015 in U.S. Dollars
Doctoral degree	1.7	1,623
Professional degree*	1.5	1,730
Master's degree	2.4	1,341
Bachelor's degree	2.8	1,137
Associate's degree	3.8	798
Some college, no degree	5.0	738
High school diploma	5.4	678
Less than a high school diploma	8.0	493
All workers	4.3	860

Per the U.S. Department of Labor, a professional degree applies to students who have attended school full time three or more years post-bachelor's degree.

Source: U.S. Department of Labor, Bureau of Labor Statistics, 2015a.

These tables illustrate the importance of helping students complete high school and become college or career ready, since the impact of education on their employment potential and earnings is so very dramatic.

The connection between education and employment also has an alarming effect on the U.S. economy. Education policy experts Tabitha Grossman, Ryan Reyna, and Stephanie Shipton (2011) observe the following:

> By 2018, it is expected that the United States will need 22 million new college degrees and at least 4.7 million new workers with postsecondary certificates but will produce 3 million fewer degrees than needed. Unfortunately, there is evidence to suggest that significant portions of the student population in the U.S. are insufficiently prepared for postsecondary education. . . . In 2011, just 25 percent of high school graduates nationwide who took the ACT standardized test scored at a level that indicates readiness for entry-level, credit-bearing college coursework without remediation in all four core subject areas. A higher percentage, about 28 percent of the U.S. students who took the ACT test met none of the readiness benchmarks. (p. 4)

Grossman et al. (2011) have contrasted the growing demand for an educated workforce with disappointing data regarding student achievement. U.S. students' low ranking on the ACT sounds a national alarm to educators, as well as to parents, since employment and earnings have connections to levels of educational attainment. The United States' traditional social mobility has declined dramatically. Niall Ferguson (2011) reports the significance of these conditions in detail:

> A compelling explanation for our increasingly rigid social system is that American public education is failing poor kids. One way it does this is by stopping them from getting to college. If your parents are in the bottom quintile, you have a 19 percent chance of getting into the top quintile with a college degree—but a miserable 5 percent chance without one.

The *Benchmarking for Success* report sounds similar warnings (NGA, CCSSO, & Achieve, 2008):

> The United States is falling behind other countries in the resource that matters most in the new global economy: human capital. . . . The U.S. ranked high in inequity, with the third largest gap in science scores between students from different socioeconomic groups. The U.S. is rapidly losing its historic edge in educational attainment as well. As recently as 1995, America still tied for first in college and university graduation rates, but by 2006 had dropped to 14th. That same year it had the second-highest college dropout rate of 27 countries. (pp. 5–6)

According to figures from the Organisation for Economic Co-operation and Development, "The U.S. has one of the highest college dropout rates in the industrialized world" (as cited in NGA et al., 2008, p. 11). That same report calls on state leaders to:

Tackle "the equity imperative" by creating strategies for closing the achievement gap between students from different racial and socioeconomic backgrounds in each of the action steps. . . . Reducing inequality in education is not only socially just, it's essential for ensuring that the United States retain a competitive edge. (p. 6)

It is clear that we, as educators, parents, and citizens, face new challenges in our efforts to recapture our former high rankings in educational attainment, employment opportunities, and economic stability. A critical piece of this *equity imperative* is adopting grading practices that are fair and clear and that give hope to students who are willing to work until their work is acceptable.

College Dropout Rates

As you've seen, educational attainment is closely connected to earning potential. Grades that students earn in high school are important not only for graduation rates but also in qualifying students for college admissions and scholarships. For example, most colleges require minimum grade point averages (GPAs) for admission; many states offer college scholarship money based on high school GPAs. Grades are therefore tied directly to earning potential. Qualifying for college admission can be challenging but is only the first step in achieving a college degree. Earning a bachelor's degree typically takes the traditional four years of class attendance (either in person, online, or a combination of the two), completion of assignments, study, exams, lab work, conferences with professors, internships, and more. But the U.S. college dropout rate after freshman year is over 30 percent, and widespread grade inflation in high schools may be a causative factor in that statistic, as students haven't truly mastered the standards necessary to excel in college (Goodwin, 2011). Grade inflation results in higher scores given for work that in the past would have earned a much lower score. Consider the following facts about grade inflation.

- Between 1991 and 2003, the mathematics and English grade point averages of students taking the ACT outpaced the rise in their ACT scores in those subjects (Woodruff & Ziomek, 2004).

- High school students' scores on the National Assessment of Educational Progress's (NAEP) reading section declined between 1992 and 2005, while students reported an upturn in grade point average between 1990 and 2005—from 2.68 in 1990 to 2.98 in 2005. In addition, the percentage of students who reported taking college-preparatory classes rose from 5 to 10 percent during that period (Schmidt, 2007).

State legislators are moving toward funding formulas based on college *graduation* rates rather than on *enrollment* rates. Funding formulas are how legislators decide how much money a state will provide its universities and colleges. In states where funding is based on graduation rates, colleges are raising selection criteria. This change may require high schools to develop grading practices that inform colleges (and students) what students have truly mastered. When high schools provide recovery credits that do not include standards-based content mastery, such as a minimum requirement for the student to pass an end-of-course test for that particular state, it can lead to students receiving diplomas they have not earned (Center for Public Education, 2012). One study found that 47 percent of students did not actually complete a college- or career-ready curriculum (Gewertz, 2016a; Gewertz, 2016b). We believe recovery credits have a place in schools, but they need to reflect some level of content mastery, not just time spent earning credits in a computer lab. Grade inflation appears to be a major factor in creating this dilemma, as is the lack of common standards on which mastery is based. Grade inflation is detrimental and misleading to students, parents, counselors, and potential employers. Should individual teachers have the freedom to determine their own grading practices when the outcomes for students are so critical? It's time now to reassess our grading policies.

Standardized Assessment

The Common Core State Standards, or similar standards codified by some states, are another reason to reconsider and improve assessment practices and policies by standardizing grading criteria. The CCSS offer teachers the opportunity to implement the kind of uniformity—while maintaining flexibility where it's needed—that can change grading practices. Having a set of common standards brings greater consistency in our grading practices, as does having common assessment approaches such as the Smarter Balanced Assessment Consortium and the Partnership for Assessment of Readiness for College and Careers, as do assessment options for students with disabilities.

Smarter Balanced Assessment Consortium and Partnership for Assessment of Readiness for College and Careers

Two different consortia, which the U.S. Department of Education funded, are implementing overall assessments of student attainment of the CCSS. Information at www.smarterbalanced.org/assessments details the plan developed for the Smarter Balanced Assessment Consortium (SBAC). Information at www.parcconline.org /assessments represents the Partnership for Assessment of Readiness for College and

Careers' (PARCC) plan. Information at www.ets.org/global relays information about standardized assessments available around the world.

SBAC and PARCC complement the CCSS and are in varying stages of implementation throughout selected states. Both offer formative and summative assessments (Grossman et al., 2011). Educators in CCSS discussions often emphasize summative assessments. Much of the controversy surrounding CCSS implementation is related to whether those summative assessments can judge or rank schools and teachers (Lenz & Kay, 2013; Wood, 2013). However, what those discussions often overlook is the value of formative assessments in guiding teaching practices in preparing *all* students to achieve grade-level content, and to successfully navigate the summative assessments. *Formative assessments* are the day-to-day or moment-to-moment impressions of student understanding, routine observations or conclusions about student mastery of skills or content, and adjustments in instruction that educator observations trigger. *Summative assessments* sum up student accomplishments and indicate mastery, and they typically take place after the usual instructional period has been completed. Summative assessments give meaning to grades because they are based on standards that are the common reference point. Therefore, grades based on summative assessments will decrease grade inflation and make college or career readiness more likely.

Various school systems have plans to implement one of these assessment approaches.

Assessment Options for Students With Disabilities

Achieve (2013) is one example of a list of CCSS assessment resources designed for use with students with disabilities. The following are different assessment resources.

- **SBAC accessibility and accommodations** (http://bit.ly/2cCxk0v) use technology to deliver assessments that fit the individual student's needs. The technology includes different colors (for readability) and Braille, American Sign Language, and other languages.

- **PARCC accessibility** (www.parcconline.org/assessments/accessibility /manual) assessment options address students with disabilities, English learners, and English learners with disabilities' needs.

- **The National Center and State Collaborative** (www.ncscpartners .org) provides assessment options based on alternative achievement standards. These assessments are for students with "the most significant cognitive disabilities" (National Center and State Collaborative, 2012).

- **The Dynamic Learning Maps Alternate Assessment System Consortium** (http://dynamiclearningmaps.org) developed an alternative assessment system for students with severe cognitive and sensory disabilities.

Since states and provinces frequently discuss and sometimes change their preferences for the various assessment organizations, check your state or province's department of education's website or school system for the most current information. You can also find a list of states and their choices on OpenEd's guide to Common Core standards (http://bit.ly/2cO2uMN; OpenEd, n.d.). The Council of Ministers of Education, Canada (www.cmec.ca) lists standards as they vary by province. (Visit **go.SolutionTree.com/instruction** to access live links to the websites mentioned in this book.)

Summary

In addition to professional reflection, a myriad of reasons make this the right time to reassess grading practices. The clear connection between education level and potential earnings and the clear risk of poverty associated with limited education are reasons to consider how we assess students. Grade inflation's link to college dropout rates is another reason, as are the opportunities schools have with standardized assessment efforts.

Reflection Questions

Use the following questions to help initiate faculty discussions and to help faculty examine the potential of changing current policies.

1. What is the primary purpose of teacher grades?

2. On what factors should teachers base grades? How important is predictability of grades? For instance, should course grades predict end-of-course test scores or the ability to perform on-the-job tasks? If important, what changes will increase predictability of a student's grade?

3. How can the practice of teaching and learning rather than sorting and selecting add meaning to grades earned by all students?

4. What are the major arguments for having both academic and non-academic reporting instruments?

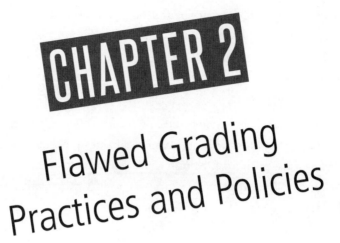

CHAPTER 2

Flawed Grading Practices and Policies

Grades convey powerful messages. Grades can encourage or discourage students and help them set goals or simply state that they failed. Educators hear many questions and opinions about grading practices and policies. Whatever differences of opinion educators encounter, Marge Scherer (2011) reminds us that:

> There is no doubt that our society believes in grades. We look for four-star movies, five-star restaurants, top-10 colleges, and even Grade A eggs. Although we tend to think of these ratings as objective, we know that it's important to read the full reviews—and look for cracks in the shells. . . . Most of us agree that if grades are going to be meaningful, they must be as accurate and fair as possible. The question before us is, How do we make that happen? (p. 7)

In an effort to create common understandings—and to find those "cracks in the shells"—before making changes, this chapter critiques several educational and grading practices: (1) sort-and-select practices, (2) seat time requirements, (3) formative and summative assessment weaknesses, and (4) skewed averages (Guskey, 2015). (The last topic is so complex that it is discussed in detail in chapter 3 on page 29.)

Sort-and-Select Practices

The policies and grading practices that most schools have followed for decades are based primarily on the sort-and-select practice (Lezotte, 2008). Typically, that process begins when students first enter school and are assigned to a grade level by age (or more specifically by birth date) and prior school experience, if any. From there, teachers assign students to instructional groups and then, at the end of each term, they make another sort-and-select decision—*pass course for credit* or *fail course* or *fail grade level*. But sort-and-select practices, on which traditional grading systems are based, do not provide sufficient flexibility given the great variety in student readiness, performance, and support.

If we expect to graduate students who qualify for college and careers, and who in turn get and keep good jobs, we must understand and support a huge paradigm shift. That is, schools must relinquish certain aspects of the old-fashioned sort-and-select practice, whose grading approach doesn't account for differentiation and focuses on deficits. Here, as a way of explaining the needed changes, we describe the issues associated with the sort-and-select practice. Chapter 4 (page 43), which discusses standards-based grading, offers remedies.

Fairness Is Not Equivalent to Sameness

Fairness is not equivalent to sameness. Robert Lynn Canady (n.d.c) notes:

> We have operated schools on the assumption that if students had to have extra support to achieve well (for example, extra time to complete a course, retake tests, or rewrite papers), then there had to be a penalty, such as averaging their low grades with their new and improved grades. This assumption is based on the belief that *fairness* is equated with *sameness*. In other words, if you want to be fair, you must treat every student the same. (p. 2)

Thus, if teachers make exceptions such as providing supplementary materials to meet an individual student's needs or allowing that student extra time to complete an assignment, they may be accused of being unfair to other students. But, rather than being unfair, those teachers are adjusting instructional methods to meet individual students' needs. Adapting content and methods to meet student needs is not new. Schools and teachers have adjusted classroom instruction through individualized education programs (IEPs) to meet special education students' individual needs. Of course, IEPs are not necessary for most students; using IEPs is simply an example of how being fair to students does not mean that every student receives the very same treatment.

In all classrooms, individual talents, varied skill levels, social development, scholarly interests, and parental support influence the instruction students need (and that teachers provide). Among students in any one classroom, some may receive a great deal of help from their parents in providing regular study time and supplying resources that aid in their studies. But other students may not even have a place to study or parents at home to provide materials, set a homework schedule, and encourage them. Thus, when teachers extend deadlines, provide supplementary materials, or offer tutoring sessions, they are simply taking into account what students need. Grading inflexibility is an issue educators need to reassess.

Assessments Focus on Deficits

The common current assessment model of sorting and selecting focuses on what students lack instead of on their potential capabilities. Pervasive grading scales have a failing range between 0 to 59 (or even up to 75). That leaves students a range of about forty points to pass, let alone in which to excel (Canady, n.d.b). The scales are tilted toward failure. It's easy to see that the range for failing is much larger than the range for passing. Standards-based grading doesn't view failure like the sort-and-select practice does. This inequity works for the sort-and-select practice but does nothing to help prepare students for college or careers.

Students Often Fail Before Getting Further Instruction

Typically, students have to perform poorly before receiving additional learning time (Canady, n.d.c). Essentially, schools have institutionalized a *take class, fail class, repeat class* instructional model. The restrictive public school schedules follow a year-long work cycle, generally consisting of between 160 and 180 school days (Canady & Rettig, 1995), and most high school classes run for single periods for all those days. Few alternative schedules are available. A failing grade often means that the student has to repeat the course instead of getting help during the first iteration. When a school's goal was primarily to sort and select students for the next level of education, and school personnel were not concerned about the number of students who dropped out or left school undereducated, a scheduling plan without alternatives may have been acceptable.

But we can no longer justify having large numbers of students spending so much time failing when we can predict such outcomes early in the course. As a result of this sort-and-select practice, in large high schools it is not unusual to identify hundreds of students who have been in high school for two or more years without having earned even ten Carnegie Units (or hours of class time with an instructor) counting toward a diploma (Rath, Rock, & Laferriere, 2012). Since the mid-1990s, about half of middle and high schools have moved to various types of flexible scheduling, including block, but few have capitalized fully on the power of creative scheduling (Canady & Rettig, 1995; Rettig & Canady, 2000). Chapter 6 (page 71) of this book details some scheduling solutions.

Seat Time Requirements

Before various types of testing became state or federal mandates, schools and systems designated scheduled times in class as the constant factor. In many schools, students are expected to meet the scheduled *seat time requirements*—a specified number of hours in class and days in school (Great Schools Partnership, 2014). In this arrangement, a student cannot earn credit unless that student meets the established seat time requirements, regardless of the prior knowledge he or she brings to class. In the United States, the seat time variable required to earn a course credit varies from 108 to 140 clock hours (Carnegie Unit and Student Hour, n.d.). Seat time worship leads to punitive attendance policies, which harm some students more than others. (Chapter 3, page 29, talks more about the students who are at higher risk.) If schools do not allow students to make up work when absent, they will receive low grades. That ultimately leads to an average grade that is impossible to overcome, discouraging and defeating those who often then miss more school.

Seat time requirements partially explain why the factor of school attendance is highly associated with dropout rates. Indeed, attendance is a critical factor in identifying which students are unlikely to earn high school diplomas (Heppen & Therriault, 2008). Many states have established various policies to free schools from the traditional seat time requirements, which the Carnegie Unit system dictates, to address such issues (Great Schools Partnership, 2014). Such policies "allow districts or schools to provide credits based on students' proving proficiency in a subject, rather than the time they physically spend in a traditional classroom setting" (Cavanagh, 2012). Removing seat time requirements can "make it easier for struggling students to catch up, exceptional students to race ahead, and students who face geographic and scheduling problems to take courses required for graduation" (Cavanagh, 2012). However, the issue is not yet entirely resolved, because some state policies, including those in Illinois and Massachusetts, prohibit or restrict alternative methods of awarding credit for actual student proficiency (Carnegie Foundation for the Advancement of Teaching [CFAT], 2014). And in nearly all states, rigid funding formulas work against implementing flexible policies for awarding credit because funding formulas are based on hours spent in class, not mastery of content (NGA, 2012).

When schools relax seat time requirements and move to standards-based grading systems, *mastery* of required material is emphasized, not just *time spent* learning the material. The issue becomes what the student can demonstrate in terms of subject mastery rather than whether he or she spent sufficient seat time in class. Therefore, if we consider *learning* as the constant factor and *time* as the variable, the equation is turned around.

Most states have already moved in this direction by permitting schools to offer flexible credits, primarily through state-approved testing options and online offerings. Such flexibility may not be granted to students, however, until they first have met the seat time requirements and failed the course at least once (CFAT, 2014). These requirements add to the problem of collecting large numbers of overage and under-credited students in high schools. Chapter 6 (page 71) outlines alternatives to seat time requirements via elementary, middle, high, and alternative school schedules that make time for students who need additional help. Now is the time to revise seat time requirements so schools can focus on flexible efforts to ensure students gain the necessary skills to be college or career ready.

Formative and Summative Assessment Weaknesses

Your school or system may not even use the terms *formative* and *summative*; yet the functions those terms denote remain important in evaluating student achievement. Certainly, teachers at all grade levels and in all subjects rely heavily on formative assessments. Formative assessments are the day-to-day or moment-to-moment impressions of student understanding, routine observations or conclusions about student mastery of skills or content, and adjustments in instruction that educator observations trigger. Formative assessment has long been familiar in classrooms at all levels and in all locations. You might even say that formative assessment is what teaching is all about. However, formative assessment is really summative if it doesn't give the appropriate feedback to students and allow them time to implement that new knowledge. Formative feedback is also flawed upon delivery in many cases. Grant Wiggins (2012) states, "Effective feedback is concrete, specific, and useful; it provides actionable information. Thus, 'Good job!' and 'You did that wrong' and B+ are not feedback at all." Homework is another way formative assessment is incorrectly applied. Recording a homework grade in the gradebook is erroneous; the student has not been asked to achieve mastery at that point. Chapter 5 (page 59) offers alternative homework policies.

On the other hand, final exams, as well as state and national tests such as the SAT and the ACT, are summative assessments. These assessments sum up student accomplishments and take place after the usual instructional period—six weeks, a semester, a grading period, an academic year, or four years—has been completed. Problems with this assessment type arise when the performance is tied to behavior (students who don't submit homework, for example, are given zeroes) and when no specific standards are tied to the summative assessment itself.

Skewed Averages

Many U.S. teachers use some form of averaging to determine summative grades, and most computer grading software is programmed to use averaging to calculate grades. Some teachers average a range of numerical scores; others place weights on letter grades and then average the various weights to arrive at a summative letter grade. Some use rubric scores of 1–4, 1–5, or even 1–10. Each calculation is a form of averaging to determine final grades.

In averaging numerical scores, the scales relating numbers to letter grades vary tremendously from one school to another. Variations exist among the methods teachers in the same building use—even in the same department. For example, some teachers average scores from 0 to 100, while some do not include scores below a certain percentage. Variations in grading scales reflect teachers', schools', and systems' differing policies and practices. Not only do inconsistencies between classes and systems cause problems when educators try to prepare students for college or a career, but averaging unevenly weighted scores also distorts grades. For example, if 70 is required to pass, weighing a low grade of 40 with a grade of 80 distorts the final grade by giving the score of 40 more power. As Canady (n.d.c) says:

> Unless we average repeated measures of similar content, a grade based on averaging loses its ability to predict. This is a major problem of end-of-course (EOC) testing and other norm-referenced measures related to educational accountability, such as Advanced Placement (AP), International Baccalaureate (IB), ACT, and SAT scores and national test standards. (p. 13)

Inconsistency and inaccuracies are also issues that affect student achievement. This chapter discusses issues in regard to zeroes, trending, and computerized averaging. Specifically, assigning a zero for work not done is punitive and disproportionately pulls averages down. Averages dismiss increased understanding by not acknowledging the grade trends (either up or down). And finally, computerized averaging doesn't allow the teacher to reflect on student improvements or contributions. Averages skew grades in various ways. The section Averaging on page 51 of chapter 4 provides solutions, such as using the median or a different average band, that address those issues and keep students engaged and achieving.

Zeroes Misrepresent Learning

Imagine averaging in the world outside school. According to Canady (n.d.b),

> Suppose we are developing a brochure for the Chamber of Commerce and our goal is to report a reliable average temperature for a week in September in Charlottesville, Virginia. The temperatures for the week, taken at noon on

Sunday, Monday, Tuesday, Wednesday, Thursday, Friday, and Saturday, were 92, 91, 90, 80, 84, 85, and 82, yielding a total of 604. If we divide 604 by 7, we get an average of 86.

Let's suppose, however, that we did not have a temperature reading for Wednesday, and we put a zero for Wednesday and still divide by 7; then we get an average of 75 (rounded from 74.8). Suppose we treated Wednesday simply as missing data and divided the total by 6 and not 7, then we would get an average of 86—no, this average should be 87 (rounded from 87.33). Which summative average is the most reliable average temperature to report to the Chamber of Commerce brochure: 75 or 86? We can see that the zero poses a problem in averaging temperatures for a week. (p. 6)

This real-world example reveals that including the zero in the averaging process is *not* a valid method for determining an average temperature, nor is it a valid way to calculate a summative grade (Guskey, 2013; Hill & Nave, 2009). The process of averaging grades distorts, camouflages, and misleads, just as including the zero in the week's temperatures throws the average off entirely.

If a score of zero represents schoolwork not done, we must develop ways of dealing with that issue (Reeves, 2004). In an age of accountability, we need assessments that will help us diagnose student needs and then provide interventions and support for students to master the standards we teach. Including zeroes in averages does not fulfill that description. Consider the case of a student who is absent twice and consequently misses two assessments. In a classroom that does not permit make-up work, the student would receive zeroes for the scores. However, in a classroom that allows or requires make-up work, the student has a better chance to earn a score reflective of his or her learning. Figure 2.1 (page 24) illustrates the effect of including zeroes in the student's average score, as well as what happens to the student's average if he or she scores 40, 50, 60, or 80 on make-up work.

Ken O'Connor and Rick Wormeli (2011) consider the influence of zeroes on a final grade both "unethical and inaccurate" (p. 41). The "digressions in [student] performance" the use of zeroes represented on the 0–100 grading scale are not indicators of a student's actual learning (O'Connor & Wormeli, 2011, p. 41). Further, the effect of zeroes is not a positive motivator to students who receive them, as O'Connor and Wormeli (2011) observe that this averaging approach "generates despair: Only a mammoth pile of perfect 100s can overcome the deficit and result in a passing *D* grade. So why bother?" (p. 41). When students know that their poor grades from the past will counteract any new grades they have achieved, they think their hard work hasn't made any difference after all. Students become discouraged and feel little motivation to keep working. Instead, students need to feel recognized and rewarded for revising and resubmitting work based on focused feedback from their teachers.

	Test 1	Test 2	Test 3	Test 4	Test 5
Student 1	72	72	72	72	72
Student 2	88	88	88	88	88
Student 3	92	92	92	92	92
Student 4	0	40	50	60	80
Student 5	66	66	66	66	66
Student 6	91	91	91	91	91
Student 7	0	40	50	60	80
Student 8	84	84	84	84	84
Student 9	87	87	87	87	87
Student 10	90	90	90	90	90
Totals	670	750	770	790	830
Averages	67	75	77	79	83

Figure 2.1: The influence of zeroes on the final grade.

Grade Order Reflects Learning Trend

A student's grades should reveal that student's learning progression. Trends, upward or downward, mostly indicate mastery or lag in sequence courses such as mathematics, foreign languages, and the writing process because the information builds on itself. If they don't understand concepts in the beginning, their grades continue to fall. Or, they might struggle at first and then catch on. The order in which a student earns grades is a factor if the school's policy mandates that teachers average several scores for a summative grade. This factor is especially important in courses taken in sequence. Averaging skews the true measure of a student's mastery in these cases. Figure 2.2 presents two students'—Alfred and Bob—sample grades during the first nine weeks of algebra 2 to illustrate difficulties with averaging the accumulated grades. The grades are based on assessments that have been given equal weight for averaging purposes. The first few weeks of algebra 2 consist of a review of the basic concepts of algebra 1, and the following weeks include new content. In fact, as much as 30 percent of algebra 2 can be a review of algebra 1. If this statement is accurate, then early in the course, a student's success may depend as much on the algebra 1 teacher as anything else.

Computer-Based Grading Strips Teacher Autonomy

Most likely, a computerized grading program calculates averages to determine summative marks or grades. Unfortunately, many problems arise when schools and systems use computerized grading programs that are based on some form of averaging. For one, like the required summative cross-semester averages, the computer averages do not take into account student improvements. It is quite possible that the computer program records students' performance early in the school year and, through the process of averaging, that information still influences the students' final grades at a semester's or school year's end. The final grades thus do not represent improvements students have made between the start and finish of the academic year. In this way, computer-based averaging emphasizes low grades' power, again skewing toward failing.

Additionally, computer assessment makes grading much less personal. Computer calculation does not take into account teachers' tabulations, records, and observations. Most computer-based grading programs will not permit grade changes after certain deadlines, which means teachers cannot reward students after those dates. Again, computerized grading programs eliminate teachers' autonomy in making decisions about grades that accurately reflect students' learning. Faculty members don't always acknowledge and parents don't always recognize these detrimental effects of computer-based averaging, but the effects may be seen in lower student motivation and achievement.

Summary

Various reasons resulted in 21st century grading practices and policies, which negatively affect student achievement. The sort-and-select practice has a host of issues—its fairness fallacy, its focus on deficiencies, and its inflexibility. Seat time requirements perpetuate sorting and selecting, rather than teaching and learning. Incorrectly administered formative and summative assessments negate the positive effects that assessments, correctly applied, can have on student achievement. Finally, averaging tends to lower student motivation and achievement. Eschew outdated sort-and-select in favor of teach-and-learn practices, which part II of this book discusses.

Reflection Questions

Use the following questions to help initiate discussions and assist faculty in examining the potential of replacing flawed grading policies and practices.

1. Whether a letter or a numerical score, what does a final grade mean when it is based on an average of a set of scores?

2. The grades of lower-achieving students, who receive grades below a C+, do not necessarily predict future failure. What can explain that?

3. What are the strengths and the weaknesses of computerized grading systems that require final grades to be determined by a specific date, with little or no flexibility to later raise the grades?

4. Which of the following factors—time, teaching, assessment, or school policy—would be the most difficult to implement in your school or district? Why?

5. What is the difference between formative and summative assessment? What would a balance of these two assessment types look like at your school or district? How do these assessment types apply to teach-and-learn versus sort-and-select practices?

6. As a high school teacher, what weight would you place on attendance, homework, classwork, and quizzes versus end-of-unit tests? Would your response differ if you were an elementary or middle school teacher? Why or why not?

7. How do traditional grading practices distinguish between formative and summative assessments?

8. What are the problems with requiring seat time when implementing a mastery learning model?

CHAPTER 3

How Poverty Creates Variables That Affect Achievement

Educators are confronted every day with the truth that students are varied and complex. Indeed, as teachers make lesson plans, student differences require as much consideration as curriculum content. Table 3.1 presents categories of student variance, elements that shape those categories, and several implications on their learning. This chapter addresses most categories and some contributors, including poverty, which are often related to geographic mobility and absenteeism and begs for better, built-in support systems.

Table 3.1: Categories of Student Variance With Implications for Learning

Category of Student Variance	Contributors to the Category	Some Implications for Learning
Biology	• Gender • Neurological proclivity to learn • Abilities • Disabilities • Development	• High ability and disability exist in a whole range of endeavors. • Students will learn in different modes. • Students will learn in different timetables. • Some parameters for learning are somewhat defined but are malleable with appropriate context and support.

continued →

Category of Student Variance	Contributors to the Category	Some Implications for Learning
Degree of privilege	• Economic status • Race • Culture • Support system • Language • Experience	• Students from low economic backgrounds and representing races, cultures, and languages not in positions of power face greater school challenges. • Quality of students' adult support system influences learning. • Breadth and depth of student experience influence learning.
Positioning for learning	• Adult models • Trust • Self-concept • Motivation • Temperament • Interpersonal skills	• Parents who actively commend education positively affect their children's learning. • Trust, positive self-concept, positive temperament, and motivation to learn positively impact student learning. • Positive interpersonal skills and emotional intelligence positively impact student learning.
Preferences	• Interests • Learning preferences • Preferences for individuals	• Student interests will vary across topics and subjects. • Student preference will vary for how to take in and demonstrate knowledge. • Students will relate to teachers differently.

Source: Tomlinson & McTighe, 2005.

Literacy and Income

The Annie E. Casey Foundation established reading at grade level by third grade a U.S. imperative; still, in 2015, about 64 percent of U.S. fourth graders performed below proficient or below grade level in reading on the Nation's Report Card (Annie E. Casey Foundation, 2010; NCES, 2015a). This statistic is especially alarming because the reading gap tends to grow larger each year a student is in school, and because catching up becomes even more difficult as content demands increase and students who are not proficient readers are ill equipped to process text at higher grade levels (Penno, Wilkinson, & Moore, 2002; Stanovich, 1986). Eighty-two percent of fourth graders reading below grade level are from low-income families (Annie E. Casey Foundation, 2010). This is related to the thirty-million-word gap.

Hart and Risley (1995) report:

The longitudinal data showed that in the everyday interactions at home, the average (rounded) number of words children heard per hour was 2,150 in the professional families, 1,250 in the working-class families, and 620 in the welfare families. . . . By age 3 the children in professional families would have heard more than 30 million words, the children in working-class families 20 million, and the children in welfare families 10 million. (pp. 132–133)

So now the link between poverty and academic achievement is no longer uncertain. "Poverty directly affects academic achievement due to the lack of resources available for student success . . . and numerous studies have documented the correlation between low socioeconomic status and low achievement" (Lacour & Tissington, 2011, p. 522). That lack of resources results in many inequities that affect academics—healthcare disparities, nutrition—not the least of which is language.

Just as the link between poverty and academic achievement is clear, so is the link between poverty and ethnicity. A disproportionate number of African American and Latino youth live in poverty. The National Center for Education Statistics (2016) reports that in 2014, 38 percent of African American and 32 percent of Latino children were living in poverty, compared to 12 percent of white children. A disproportionate number of African American and Latino students also have lower levels of academic achievement. For example, the average score for African American and Latino fourth graders was more than 20 points lower than white fourth graders' on the 2015 National Assessment of Educational Progress (NAEP) reading test (NCES, 2015a). The test takers included approximately 279,000 fourth graders from public and private schools across the United States (NCES, 2015b).

From the beginning of their lives, youth in poverty are at a disadvantage. Their support at home doesn't provide for school readiness and their achievement lags from the beginning, leading to bigger dropout rates and, in turn, higher poverty. That cycle is strongly entrenched, and high-quality education is the key to breaking children born into poverty out of it (Rothstein, 2014). Revamping our grading practices can help provide that high-quality education. Educators need to focus on strategies like those in part II of this book to increase all students' academic achievements, beginning in preK and kindergarten. It can be argued that such a goal should be a priority.

Geographical Mobility

For students, moving to a new home often means moving to a new school with different courses and different grading practices. But in states where the CCSS are in place, students are likely to find learning goals and grading practices similar to those in the schools they moved from. That's why family mobility is an important reason for implementing common standards (Common Core State Standards Initiative, n.d.a; Ihrke & Faber, 2012).

Is mobility really important? The U.S. Department of Commerce periodically measures and reports the population's geographical mobility, because population shifts affect all functions of all levels of government, as well as private industries (Ihrke & Faber, 2012). Population type, such as (1) within the same county, (2) from a different county in the same state, (3) from a different state, or (4) from abroad, is generally used to classify population shifts. Highlights from the population survey's December 2012 report find that:

- People in their mid- to late twenties had the highest mover rate of 65.5 percent.

- Unemployed individuals (47.7 percent) were more mobile than their employed (civilian) counterparts (37.2 percent).

- Between 2005 and 2010, the South was the only region to report a significant net gain of 1.1 million due to migration. (Ihrke & Faber, 2012, p. 1)

Note that the most people moving are in their mid- to late twenties. This group no doubt includes many young parents whose children are likely to be moving from school to school. Further, this survey reports that "People employed by the Armed Forces had the highest mover rate of any employment status, with 72.7 percent"; this percentage includes "only members of the Armed Forces living off post or with their families on post in the United States" but does not include military families stationed outside the United States (Ihrke & Faber, 2012, p. 6). Of course, if your school serves military families, you are no doubt aware of the coming and going of their children. However, the issue of mobility is not limited to military families. More than one-third of the general population in the United States relocates every five years or so (Ihrke & Faber, 2012). Migrant labor accounts for students changing schools, as well; many of these students are at a double disadvantage because they are English learners (Kindler, 1995).

Throughout the United States, family relocations affect huge numbers of students; therefore, mobility is a pervasive and constant influence on our efforts to improve grading practices (Astone & McLanahan, 1994). If we can implement common reference points and match grading practices among teachers and schools, we can expect to improve student achievement and test scores.

Absenteeism and Dropout Rates

A large percentage of students will experience failure at an early age, and chronic absenteeism is a major factor in that failure (Chang & Romero, 2008). As noted, state policies requiring seat hours regardless of mastery are problematic. According to Hedy Chang (2010), 10 percent of U.S. kindergarteners and first graders miss at least one month of school and fall behind their classmates; this is known as *chronic absenteeism*. Students miss school for a variety of reasons including housing instability, family obligations, illness, and harassment avoidance (Balfanz & Byrnes, 2012). Economically disadvantaged students are more likely to experience some of these factors, which helps explain why chronic absentee rates are significantly higher among these students (Balfanz & Byrnes, 2012). Attendance predicts whether students will complete high school, particularly if they are absent frequently during middle school and ninth grade and during the first thirty days of a school year (Allensworth & Easton, 2007). Similarly, research scientists Ruth Curran Neild and Robert Balfanz (2006) indicate that failing ninth grade is a key predictor of dropping out.

Measuring attendance for individual students in a school is entirely different from reporting average daily attendance for the school or the system as a whole. For example, "A school can have average daily attendance of 90 percent and still have 40 percent of its students chronically absent, because on different days, different students make up that 90 percent" (Balfanz & Byrnes, 2012, p. 3). Chronic absenteeism is "more prevalent among high-poverty students" (Resmovits, 2012), and chronically absent students tend to be concentrated in a subset of schools. For example, Balfanz and Byrnes (2012) report that 15 percent of Florida schools are responsible for 50 percent or more students who are chronically absent. Regardless of age, gender, and ethnic background, when students do not attend school regularly, they cannot acquire the necessary skills that prepare them to succeed in school. Failure at an early age erases students' confidence and lowers the likelihood of achievement. Certain factors related to absenteeism, such as family mobility, become less relevant when schools focus on a common reference point created by standards-based grading. Mastery of common content rather than seat time becomes the focus of teaching, learning, and grading.

Over the years, schools have built grading policies and practices primarily on the theory that fear of failure will motivate students to succeed. Fear of failure will indeed motivate *some* students—primarily those who are doing well in school. However, once students experience repeated incidents of failure, they often begin to believe they cannot be academically successful. Students often seem to find ways to fulfill that prophecy or at least pretend not to care and often not to try again. Thus, fear of failure does not motivate all students (Stiggins, 2004, 2007).

One of the easiest ways for human beings to avoid responsibility for failure is to quit trying. It's human nature to protect ourselves from hurt and embarrassment. When given a choice, we tend to stay in our comfort zones. However, as we mature and gain successful experiences and become confident, we become more willing to take risks and to expose our vulnerabilities. Such risk taking is less likely among young people who experience little or no success in school and, therefore, have come to believe they cannot be academically successful. Students, depending on age and degree of hostility, may not articulate why they will not try to perform in school, but their behavior may tell the story. For example, a student may say to the teacher, or at least to him- or herself, "Hey, Teach, I did not fail your test yesterday because I did not take your test! In fact, I didn't come to school yesterday because I knew you were going to give the test." Chapter 6 (page 71), in part II, proposes scheduling variations that can help minimize or offset student absenteeism.

Educators can offer support services that combat this negative mindset. Significant improvements in our students' achievement, especially those who have little or no support at home, are more likely when they feel their teachers genuinely care. In a major study in Chicago Public Schools, Elaine M. Allensworth and John Q. Easton (2008) find that students attend class more frequently and achieve greater success when:

- Students have strong relationships with their teachers
- Students understand that school and their courses are important to their futures
- Students feel their peers support their academic success

Summary

Poverty itself has far-reaching implications for students, including learning readiness, vocabulary, and absenteeism. Geographic mobility can be related to poverty and highlights the need for consistency among grading practices. The lack of grading consistencies prevalent in traditional grading practices, combined with limited support outside of school, creates a critical need for supportive school environments. Achievement and success become much more likely when schools provide the solutions presented in part II of this book.

Reflection Questions

Use the following questions to help initiate faculty discussions and assist faculty to examine the potential of standards-based grading.

1. How can adopting a set of universal curricular standards be a positive factor for students whose families move multiple times during their early school years?

2. Why is literacy acceleration in the early grades so critical for children entering school with multiple literacy deficits?

3. Why is it important to build student supports into the master schedule?

4. There is ample evidence that poverty is related to school absenteeism. How can standards-based grading and scheduled school supports benefit students with high levels of absenteeism?

5. If standards-based grading arguably increases levels of student mastery, how does this assumption affect students living in poverty and who have limited support outside of school?

Implement Solutions to the Problems

PART II

Schools can move toward solutions to the problems archaic grading systems present and variables such as poverty exacerbate. However, educators must know the differences between sort-and-select and teach-and-learn practices. Table P.1 compares sort-and-select and teach-and-learn approaches to four factors: (1) time, (2) instruction, (3) assessment, and (4) school policy.

Table P.1: Educational Factors Associated With Sort-and-Select and Teach-and-Learn Practices

TIME FACTORS		
Educational Factors	**Sort and Select**	**Teach and Learn**
Learning time	Is equal for all	Varies according to need
Time per course	Is equal for all	Varies according to standard and level of mastery required
Interventions	Provided after course	Provided before, during, and after course
Teacher workload	Focuses on the number of minutes or periods teachers teach and how many students are in each class (Ouchi, 2009)	Focuses on the number of students for whom a teacher can realistically provide focused feedback and support (Ouchi, 2009)
Student workload	Centers on how many credits a student takes at any one period of time	Centers on how much concurrent learning a student can master and how educators can reduce failing time
Grouping	Bases itself on semester, year-long, or course-long tracking	Bases itself on level of mastery; is flexible and temporary
Course repeats	Has student repeat whole course	Has student repeat course faster or selected concepts in course
Degrees of failure	Has student repeat whole course regardless of the degree of failure	Has student repeat only those concepts which have not been mastered

INSTRUCTION FACTORS		
Educational Factors	**Sort and Select**	**Teach and Learn**
Work revision	Is not permitted	Encourages and expects revision until students master course content
Responsibility for learning	Has teacher cover the material; students have an opportunity to learn it	Has teacher and students share responsibility for student learning
Cooperative learning and peer tutoring	Opposes using students as peer tutors	Uses students as peer tutors to meet high levels of achievement; students who help others are also learning
Individual attention	Offers little time for individual attention; uses mean scores to measure success	Mandates individual attention; uses passing rate to judge success
Resource teachers	Views resource teachers as interfering with class routines	Views resource teachers as needed aid for student success
Readiness for learning	Believes it's the parent or guardian (home) responsibility	Believes it's a shared responsibility
Materials for learning	Believes home and student should provide materials	Believes all parties share responsibility
Make-up work	Reduces credit, if accepted	Permits and supports make-up work to support student learning
Test retake	Is not permitted	Permits and encourages; mastery is the goal
ASSESSMENT FACTORS		
Educational Factors	**Sort and Select**	**Teach and Learn**
Purpose of assessment	Sorts and selects; assessments are primarily *of* learning, not *for* learning	Identifies who has mastered course objectives, who needs more time to learn, and what the teacher needs to reteach
Content of assessment	Lacks clearly articulated expectations for learning and the concepts or skills test will cover	Delineates and aligns curriculum standards with tests

continued ➜

Grading timetable	Includes formative and summative grading	Includes formative feedback; summative grading
Content of grade	Factors in academic compliance and behavior	Factors in academic compliance only; reports behavior separately
Knowledge of students' progress	Is teacher controlled	Is common knowledge and shared information throughout the school and system
Reporting to parents	Ranks the student compared to other students	Explains how the student has mastered required standards
Conferences	Teacher communicates to parent or guardian	Teacher communicates with parent or guardian and student

SCHOOL POLICY FACTORS		
Educational Factors	**Sort and Select**	**Teach and Learn**
Attendance	Fails student automatically when the student reaches a certain absence threshold	Offers opportunities and support for student to make up missed school time and complete missed assignments
Tardiness	May count student as absent if he or she is tardy	Protects class time; students pay comp time for tardies
Grades on transcript	All grades for repeated courses recorded on the transcript	Students may repeat a course for a higher grade, which replaces the lower grade on the transcript
Class rank	Allows student to manipulate system and choose courses based on their positive effect on class rank	Allows students to take courses based on interest or the potential contribution to career readiness and college preparation
Transcript versus report card	Uses both instruments to serve the same purpose	Uses report cards to explain progress and missteps to students and parents; uses transcript to relay the student's content mastery to prospective employers and colleges

Per table P.1, you can conclude that standards-based grading aligns with the teach-and-learn practice because standards-based grading works on the assumption that most students can master content given sufficient time, focused feedback, and support. Standards-based grading is largely related to product criteria because it provides evidence that documented learning has occurred. The table may also help staff assess how they can implement various factors in their own schools. Of course, the entire range of changes can be intimidating. Teachers and principals jointly decide when and how to move strategically and successfully from the sort-and-select practice to teach-and-learn practice.

Fortunately, many schools are now moving toward standards-based grading and reconsidering the negative effects of averaging. They also are rethinking homework policies and the role homework should play in determining a summative grade. If these changes are implemented with fidelity, it is reasonable to conclude that the number of discipline referrals will decrease and student attendance and graduation rates will increase. We'll investigate these solutions in the following chapters.

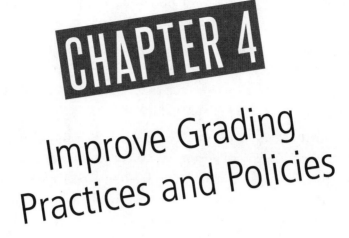

Improve Grading Practices and Policies

Chapter 2 focuses on flawed, dated teaching and grading practices. This chapter details some alternatives that schools have to those approaches. Typically, districts are expected to conform to state or provincial and local grading scales, although individual teachers sometimes apply their own judgment and adapt grading scales independently to meet their students' needs. Still, the grading policies and practices states and school systems require often follow the traditions that have been in use for many years. Thomas R. Guskey (2011) characterizes such long-held grading traditions as grading reform road blocks that do not coincide with efforts to improve education since the late 2000s. The following chapters explain standards-based grading, averaging, and homework.

Standards-Based Grading

The Common Core State Standards and other standards make it easier for school districts to move *away* from traditional grading practices and *toward* standards-based grading. Educators can base grades on common reference points—standards—that make it possible to develop uniform grading policies and standards, resulting in less variability among teachers and schools and focusing on content mastery. Successful standards-based grading implementation requires additional changes as well. A major change for schools in moving to standards-based grading is that parents, administration, and faculty must view student failure very differently than they do traditionally. Although challenging to implement, standards-based grading requires that educators view failure as an opportunity for learning when students have the necessary time, focused feedback, and support, rather than viewing failure as inevitable for a certain percentage of students (*The Huffington Post*, 2008; Reeves, 2008).

Danny Hill and Jayson Nave (2009) insist that we must change the notion that a student is in trouble or should be ashamed because he or she needs more time or more help. In addition, we have to erase the idea that if a student doesn't finish the work in class, he or she has to work on it at home.

Table 4.1 clearly summarizes the differences between traditional and standards-based grading. Traditional grading is based on a sort-and-select model of identifying students who have mastered various levels of expected content (O'Connor, 2011). The contrasts make it easy to understand standards-based grading's advantages, such as eliminating reports on conduct from subject grades. Content mastery must be separated from behavior (à la product, process, and progress criteria).

Table 4.1: Traditional Versus Standards-Based Grading System

Traditional Grading	Standards-Based Grading
Traditional grading is based on assessment methods; one grade per subject is given.	Standards-based grading is based on learning goals with a grade for each goal.
Traditional grading is based on a percentage system. It is often norm referenced, and criteria are unclear.	Standards-based grading employs criterion-referenced and proficiency-based criteria using a limited number of levels with criteria and targets known to all.
Traditional grading uses an uncertain mix of achievement, attitude, effort, and behavior. Traditional grading uses penalties and extra credit.	Standards-based grading only measures achievement; teachers report behaviors separately. No penalties or bonuses are given.
Traditional grading includes group scores.	Standards-based grading only includes individual evidence.
Traditional grading scores may include everything, regardless of purpose.	Standards-based grading only uses summative assessments.
Traditional grading includes every score regardless of when it was collected.	Standards-based grading emphasizes the more recent evidence of learning.
Traditional grading calculates the mean for grades.	Standards-based grading calculates grades using median, mode, and professional judgment.
Assessments vary in quality. Some evidence may come only from teacher recollection.	Standards-based grading employs only quality assessment and carefully recorded data.
The teacher makes decisions about grading and announces these decisions to students.	The teacher discusses all aspects of grading with students.

Source: Adapted from O'Connor, 2011.

Traditional grading approaches don't separate product, process, and progress criteria, which may account for misapplying formative and summative assessments in many classrooms. The following sections explain how to separate product, process, and progress criteria from each other and clarify how, and if, each can be graded to more accurately assess student learning.

Separate Product, Process, and Progress Criteria

Most teachers consider at least three sets of criteria when determining grades: (1) product, (2) process, and (3) progress. *Product criteria* refer to student mastery of selected materials, which often is determined using a one hundred–point scale. *Process criteria* refer to students' nonacademic behaviors, sometimes reported as *deportment* or *conduct*. *Progress criteria* refer to measurements of improvement in learning from one point in time to another (Guskey, 2006). These criteria are weighted or valued differently depending on the teacher, the discipline or subject, the school, and the student (Guskey, 1996, 2006, 2011; Guskey & Jung, 2006; Jung & Guskey, 2010). For example, a mathematics teacher may place more value than an art teacher on product criteria, who may consider progress criteria more important.

Regardless of the way (or if) teachers weight these factors, Guskey (2011) recommends using separate grades for product, process, and progress criteria, and we agree with him. In fact, standards-based grading requires that the focus of the summative grade be on product factors. Process factors are critical but need to be dealt with separately from product and progress factors. For example, an employability scale may indicate to a future employer that a student has mastered required skills, which relate to product factors, but also show evidence of poor attendance, tardiness, and incomplete homework assignments—all behaviors typically related to process factors. Indeed, educators must ask themselves whether they teach nonacademic behaviors—especially since 21st century grading practices build in those behaviors. Still, the challenge in reporting multiple grades is that clear definitions of the indicators related to product, process, and progress criteria are absolutely necessary and that the definitions must be clearly communicated to students, parents, and others (Guskey, 2011). The following sections explore these three sets of criteria in more detail.

Product Criteria

Product criteria are similar to summative assessments, since both terms' definitions include end-of-unit tests or projects, final exams, and state and national tests. As Canady (n.d.c) and Guskey and Jung (2006) indicate, the following factors address whether the student can, at a specific point in time:

- Demonstrate a level of mastery of selected material
- Meet established course expectations

- Perform a skill sufficiently

- Complete an acceptable project based on established criteria

- Pass tests with sufficient scores that indicate mastery

Product grades usually follow a one hundred–point scale whose flaws are explained in part I of this book: skewed averaging and combining behaviors (such as not accepting late homework because it is considered "irresponsible") with academic grades. Product assessments used in standards-based grading require that teachers inform students of learning targets at the beginning of the class and make it clear what evidence of learning—what products—they'll accept. Examples of product assessments include a research paper that meets the requirements of predetermined assignment criteria, passing a test designed to measure mastery of a particular concept or skill, or a project completed according to established criteria designed to illustrate mastery of the designed learning goals. By making clear what counts toward a grade, teachers eliminate secrecy from their assessments and increase students' chances to improve their performance (Guskey & Jung, 2006).

Process Criteria

Canady (n.d.c) and Guskey (2006) assert that process criteria factors are student behaviors. For example, did the student do the following?

- Follow directions

- Complete all assignments on time

- Come to class on time

- Attend the required number of classes

Process criteria influence teachers to varying degrees. Process criteria "relate to power and control issues within the classroom or the school under the name of 'teaching students to be responsible'" (Canady, n.d.a). In other words, process criteria highly value student compliance in determining success. Frequently, process criteria are independent of what the student has done—but often depend on the support system provided to the student, both in and out of school. For example, it is not unusual to find schools that will accept a late project or paper, but only if there is a penalty, such as a lowered product grade. Proponents of standards-based grading argue the mixing of process and product factors unfairly distorts the product grade. Some teachers let students retake tests, but only if the new grade is averaged with the old grade. Teachers often mix product and process factors in an attempt to prepare students for the working world.

The mixing of product and process factors unfairly impacts students who lack support outside of school. Success may also depend on the teacher having taught the behavior he or she is evaluating. The Center for Research on Teaching and Learning (n.d.) at the University of Michigan reports that "Students' success in college is influenced by their use of effective study skills." Canady (n.d.c) asserts that the teacher must do with the process behaviors what he or she does with the academic standards: make them explicit, teach them, and specify what is considered appropriate evidence of learning. That requires objective, not subjective, criteria.

Progress Criteria

Progress criteria are related to learning improvement. These include progress from one point in time to another—for example, from one lab experiment to another or from one test to another when it covers similar content. Documented behavior improvements count as progress criteria as well. This kind of approach diverges dramatically from the sort-and-select practice and moves into the teach-and-learn practice. A grade based on an individual student's progress over a specified time period can increase student motivation and, hence, achievement (Canady, n.d.b; Stiggins, 2004). However, because there is subjectivity to these criteria, some grading and scheduling flexibility may be required (Canady, n.d.b). This means that the time factor, including focused feedback and student support, has to adjust to allow continuous progress to occur. Chapter 6 (page 71) offers schedules that adjust time variables for elementary, middle, and high schools.

When progress criteria are built into grades along with mastery learning strategies—standards-based grading—students tend to receive higher grades since they attain credit for their repeated efforts to improve. Standards-based grading is built on the concept of mastery learning. Grades should have meaning; when we build in factors other than product factors, grades lose meaning (Scriffiny, 2008). When progress criteria are built into grades, teachers "may be accused of inflating grades, when in reality the improved grades occur because the teacher/school implemented research-based teaching and learning strategies and relied less on sorting and selecting practices" (Canady, n.d.b, p. 5; Scriffiny, 2008).

Implement Standards-Based Grading Realistically

Repeated discussions among faculty and administration are required to change to standards-based grading, including question-and-answer sessions, comparisons with other schools' results, and faculty trials of the new approach, followed by periodic progress evaluations. In other words, it takes time.

Typically, fully implementing standards-based grading takes at least three years—and it may take longer, particularly in high schools (Donen, Anton, Beard, Stinson, & Sullivan, 2010; *The Huffington Post*, 2008). Fairview High School in Fairview, Tennessee, moved to standards-based grading in stages over a period of five years (Donen et al., 2010). Fairview's principal Tony Donen and colleagues (2010) note that as his school year progressed, the staff focused on changing the normal categories of tests, then homework, and so on into standards. For another example, elementary schools in Lawrence, Kansas, moved gradually to standards-based grading (Fagan, 2011). For a few years, fourth- and fifth-grade teachers gave their students letter grades as well as standards-based forms. In 2011, these teachers began to use only the standards-based forms. However, sixth graders continued to receive both letter grades and the standards-based forms. At each grade level and for each subject, the standards reflect Kansas state standards. Figure 4.1 offers one option for reporting standards-based grading. The highest rating appears at the bottom of the list to avoid creating the expectation that every student should get an E.

S	Successfully meets standards
M	Making progress
T	Targeted for growth
E	Excels consistently

Figure 4.1: Reporting standards-based grading option.

The standards-based grade reports that students and parents received in Lawrence, Kansas, go beyond content learning. They also include a section regarding learner behaviors such as study skills and homework preparation. These types of assessments serve as diagnostic information for student, parent, and teacher planning about how to bring the student's achievement up to par.

Standards-based grading, which several school districts in Minnesota adopted, focuses on student mastery of Minnesota's academic standards, using a 1 to 4 scale (Koumpilova, 2013). The scale numbers correspond to the four possible outcomes on state achievement tests, which figure 4.2 shows.

1	Does not meet standards
2	Partially meets standards
3	Meets standards
4	Exceeds standards

Figure 4.2: Reporting standards-based grading option.

Students frequently receive extra opportunities to master the material covered in classes, and final grades do not include early stumbles in mastering content. Traditional numerical grades are also used, designed to show how well students have mastered the concepts in their courses. Students can retake tests and resubmit assignments, and the most recent grade, not an average, prevails in reports and records (Donen et al., 2010; Koumpilova, 2013).

At Ramsey Middle School in Minneapolis, Minnesota, principal Paul Marietta reports that he is "encouraged to see more students meeting with teachers before classes or on their lunch breaks to prep for do-overs" (Koumpilova, 2013). The Osseo Area Schools in Minnesota began standards-based grading in 2011 and, in their second year of standards-based grading across all grades, teachers saw fewer Ds and Fs but also fewer As; and the patterns of scoring on the state mastery tests were rather unexpected. For example, eighth graders who got Bs in mathematics on their report cards "scored all over the spectrum from *does not meet standards* to *exceeds standards* on the state [mathematics] test" (Koumpilova, 2013). This example illustrates why all stakeholders must understand the criteria for establishing standards-based grading. When grades are based on mastery and not mixed with process factors, it is not unusual for students who previously received high grades to receive lower grades because grades are no longer based on process compliance.

Address Opposition to Standards-Based Grading

In some school districts, school board members and central office staff oppose standards-based grading (Koumpilova, 2013; Skyward, n.d.). Furthermore, parents of high-achieving students in traditional grading programs sometimes oppose changing to standards-based grading, especially when their children have demonstrated success with traditional grading practices. As if classroom learning were similar to an athletic contest, some opponents of standards-based grading are convinced that winners cannot exist without losers. Through the years, the sort-and-select grading schemes have bolstered such thinking.

Becoming a responsible student is a learned behavior, and simply failing students does not teach them responsibility. One way to set students on a path to independent, competent learning is to gradually release responsibility for learning from teacher to student (Fisher & Frey, 2008). With the goal of independent learning, this process requires teachers to provide students with varying levels of support. That would begin with higher levels such as direct instruction and modeling, followed by gradual reduction such as guided instruction, peer collaboration, and independent practice (Fisher & Frey, 2008).

Use Modified Standards-Based Grading

As your school prepares to implement standards-based grading, you may find it helpful to begin with modified standards-based grading. *Modified standards-based grading* is, quite simply, a form of diagnostic instruction where teachers analyze student errors on assessments and assignments, reteach the necessary skills until students master them, and manage grading and scoring to keep students working diligently to master the material. Modified standards-based grading differs from true standards-based grading because the former allows some penalty for students who have to continue working to master content. Though this model violates the primary principles of standards-based grading, it is the only model that is accepted in some schools. Ultimately, schools can implement true standards-based grading after accepting the modified standards-based grading model. Modification includes the following nine steps.

1. Give a practice test as assessment *for* learning (formative) like an informal reading inventory (Stiggins, 2004).

2. Teach or reteach whatever skills, concepts, content, procedures, and principles were identified as *needing improvement* on the assessment *for* (formative) learning (Stiggins, 2004).

3. With this diagnostic information, provide an assessment *of* learning (summative) to determine the student's progress in learning the retaught material (Stiggins, 2004).

4. At first, enter only scores of 80 percent or higher in the gradebook. For scores less than or equal to 79 percent, enter only I (incomplete), NG (no grade), or E (extended time given). Keep the temporary grades until the student's retest shows mastery.

5. Continue reteaching and providing extra help or interventions as needed.

6. Retest each concept not yet mastered. Provide one retest in class or during school hours, and provide one more retest after school or at some time other than regular school hours.

7. Record retest scores of less than or equal to 80 percent in the gradebook as 80 percent (replacing any grades of I, NG, or E). Teachers occasionally will accept the limit of 80 percent rather than the full new score.

8. After retests are exhausted, record the score from the most recent retest in the gradebook.

9. Organize and grade final exams by concepts or standards mastered. They serve as the last retest opportunity for students who have not yet mastered the standards being taught (less than 80 percent). Scores on the final exam, if higher, replace previously recorded scores (less than 80 percent). The overall final exam score is recorded in the gradebook as a single entry.

In addition, the process of modified standards-based grading must establish how many reassessments can occur and how much study time must be scheduled after school or outside school hours at the onset of implementation. In this plan, based on formative assessments, reteaching and retesting are natural, normal steps to take when students do not quickly and easily demonstrate the desired proficiency in learning subject matter. Thus, teachers give struggling students opportunities to learn the required content, improve their test scores, and meet established grade-level goals.

Averaging

Chapter 2 details myriad ways averaging, though common, doesn't accurately reflect student achievement. Here we address what different approaches teachers can try if they must use averages. Ken O'Connor and Rick Wormeli (2011) suggest teachers use a single grading scale with clear definitions and limits, such as 1, 2, 3, and 4 (see figure 4.2, page 48). With grading scales such as this, all scores have equal influence on a student's overall score and thus represent a more accurate report of that student's mastery. That accurate reflection helps prevent grade inflation and potential college dropout. Achievement increases when mastery is the focus.

Or teachers can try another averaging approach. Using the median reduces the influence of extreme scores (Wright, 1994). Alternately, Rick Wormeli (2006) recommends that we turn "zeroes to sixty" and adjust the grade ranges to keep students within the "recoverable end" of the F range (p. 140). Changing 0s into 60s does not automatically give the student a passing grade average. It does, however, make it much more likely that a student can recover a passing average. Then the student can redo whatever the assignment was and try to earn a better grade to replace the 60 percent score. Motivation is the major issue; the goal is to keep students working and believing they can recover from initial failure.

Now and then teachers object to equalizing the range of scores on the grading scale and giving students opportunities to make up missed or failed work on the grounds that students don't deserve a second chance. Teachers may tell students, as a rationale for failing to provide a chance to make up work, that they won't get second chances in the real world. But that threat is simply erroneous. We all get second chances, and third, and fourth, and so on, throughout our lives. What if we mark the wrong box on a legal form? We make the correction and initial it. What about the farmer who has to replant the soybeans after a storm that floods the fields? What about those who make second or third marriages? Even the Internal Revenue Service will accept reasonable requested delays in income tax return filings. And if you don't score well on the bar exam, you can sign up to take it again. It is far more realistic to teach students that mistakes do happen and that they must continue trying after failure. We can make it possible for them to keep trying, with extra support if necessary, until they succeed. If we want students to succeed, it is important to "grade in pencil"— to give students opportunities to improve their learning and their grades—as long as possible. Intensive Care Unit (ICU) is an approach that helps teachers grade in pencil. Learn more about ICU, which focuses on quality assignments and grading, at Power of ICU (www.poweroficu.com). (Visit **go.SolutionTree.com/instruction** to access live links to the websites mentioned in this book.) ICU's creators, Jayson Nave and Danny Hill, suggest ways teachers can get students to complete every assignment. Some of these suggestions follow.

- Building intervention or enrichment periods into the master schedule

- Using time before and after school and during lunch to help students complete all assignments

- Occasionally removing students from various classes to work on other content

- Assigning students personal supports

- Having a uniform messaging system that keeps parents, students, and teachers informed of what students need to do and how school personnel are assisting

Homework

No book on grading practices would be complete without discussing homework and its relation to grades. When a school is considering moving to standards-based grading, homework may be the most controversial issue, at least with the teachers. Systemwide policies rarely attempt to ensure time allotments and types of homework assignments for all the various grade levels and subjects. Consequently, teachers within the same school and the same grade may have different approaches. This makes consistency in homework assignments across grade levels and throughout systems a major challenge. Alfie Kohn (2006, 2007) casts grave doubt on the commonly expected benefits of homework. Sort-and-select tradition asserts that homework is a necessary variable in the learning process. Kohn (2007) finds "absolutely no evidence of any academic benefit from assigning homework in elementary or middle school" (p. 36). Instead, he identifies three negative effects of homework: (1) student frustration, (2) lack of time for other activities, and (3) the often unwanted role of enforcer for parents. All those decrease motivation. Lack of motivation affects achievement. Even for high school students, the correlation between homework and achievement is very weak and "tends to disappear when more sophisticated statistical measures are applied" (Kohn, 2007, p. 36). Despite the lack of positive results, homework assignments have increased since the 1900s. Kohn (2007) recommends teachers familiarize themselves with the evidence regarding homework's varied effects and sharing the information with other teachers, parents, and central office administrators so everyone can begin rethinking standardized homework policies. Teachers can (Kohn, 2007):

- Make homework assignments only when they're truly necessary, reflecting on whether homework will help students think deeply about questions that matter

- Become informed about the difficulties some students may have in completing homework and consider this information when designing homework

- See homework as a form of formative assessment, providing feedback to both teacher and student (Vatterott, 2015)

- Move away from building homework grades into summative or final grades

The following sections discuss assigning very little homework and ensuring that assignments are student driven, and choosing not to grade homework.

Assign Scarce, Student-Driven Homework

Kohn (2007) recommends teachers assign only homework that they design, and urges them to create assignments that align with different student interests and capabilities. Motivation, and hence achievement, increase when there is student buy-in. To that end, Kohn (2007) suggests using homework to involve students in decision making. Conduct class discussions about what students are interested in learning more about and how they can answer their own questions.

Another homework studies expert, Harris Cooper, has distilled analyses into useful principles that boost student achievement, though he warns that pro- and antihomework advocates can find studies that support their positions (Cooper, 2006; Cooper, Robinson, & Patall, 2006). Homework appears to be more effective with high schoolers than with elementary and middle school students. As different variables (such as home support, socioeconomic status, student ability, quality of instruction, and motivation) are *controlled* for, or made even, the correlation between homework and achievement, other than teacher grades, diminishes (Cooper, 2006; Cooper et al., 2006). These studies suggest that for many students, homework has limited value in boosting achievement.

Cooper (2006) also recommends that homework boosts student achievement if it is limited by time spent. The general rule is ten minutes times the grade level, although encouraging and rewarding daily reading is always appropriate. No achievement gain is reached if middle school students complete more than an hour and a half of homework. Achievement begins to decline after two and a half hours of homework per night for high school students. Cooper (2006) says homework should be considered a formative assessment that lets teachers check for understanding to help readjust often incorrectly applied assessments.

Another alternative homework approach is evidenced in Kings Local School District in Kings Mills, Ohio (Canady, 2013). J.F. Burns Elementary School developed a consistent, feasible homework plan for grades K–4 that administrators explain during its parent orientation sessions at the beginning of the school year. Mathematics homework is due on Wednesdays, social studies and science homework on Thursdays, and language arts and reading homework on Fridays. The quality and completion of homework increases when schools balance the workload and systematize homework responsibilities. The Kings Mills plan gives balance to homework and allows parents and students to make plans for completing homework while also participating in other family activities.

Decide Whether to Grade Homework

Vatterott (2009) suggests that educators consider homework a source of formative feedback for students, and that function can change educators' perspective on grading homework assignments. As teachers check student work on assignments, they will naturally be judging how well students are learning the content or skills. Then, based on what they learn from these formative assessments, teachers can judge how much more practice students need in order to attain mastery. Grading homework is not necessary to evaluate mastery understanding. In fact, grading these efforts can be detrimental to the students' motivation to learn.

If teachers insist on grading homework, they can consider separating product, process, and progress criteria, as noted previously. Teachers report that providing a separate grade for homework makes "students take homework assignments more seriously" (Guskey, 2011). Another approach to ensure success with homework is to create time limits for completion. For example, the teacher can provide a list of questions or assignments and then explain that students should spend thirty minutes answering the list, but no more. Teachers can prioritize assignments if flexibility is needed, giving directions such as "do the reading first, then math" or "spend at least ten minutes on each subject" (Vatterott, 2010, pp. 13–14). Of course, teachers can also simply limit homework assignments to one or two subjects per night, aligning those assignments with newly introduced content or emphasizing major concepts for review before testing.

Peg Dawson (n.d.) describes daily routines that can assist parents and families in managing homework expectations and help students establish lifelong organizational skills. You and your faculty may reiterate to parents the importance of establishing a consistent homework time, place, and approach. Dawson (n.d.) also describes approaches for parents and students facing homework assignments. Parents can (1) assure their child that he or she will get to do his or her favorite activities as soon as he or she completes the homework, (2) offer their child homework points for doing his or her homework, which can be redeemed for privileges, (3) let their child take a break—as often as every fifteen minutes if necessary, and (4) let the child choose what assignment to complete first. Options take personal preferences into account. Completing homework is the standard in this case; giving each student some choice about how he or she will complete the assignment increases motivation.

Some educators balk when presented with the idea of not grading homework, but the issue of grading homework becomes moot with standards-based grading. Standards-based grading asks for documented evidence that the student has mastered the material (or requires additional instruction and practice).

According to Adam V. Maltese, Robert H. Tai, and Xitao Fan (2012), homework assignments may serve as better preparation for taking standardized tests than for remembering subject matter presented in class. One possible explanation is that spending more time on homework provides students with exposure to the kinds of questions and the ways of answering those questions that are similar to standardized tests. Maltese et al. (2012) recommend that educators consider all the demands on students' time and assign clear, focused homework assignments. Educators should strive for quality, not quantity of work.

Summary

Moving away from the sort-and-select practice brings educators toward standards-based grading. Standards-based grading clarifies learning targets and ensures that process criteria (most often behavior expectations, not academics) are separate and explicit. Standards-based grading also requires a different approach to averaging, which can cause student motivation to suffer and prevent teachers from seeing a student's achievement trends. A different approach to homework is necessary here as well. Take an altered approach—limiting time, alternating days or singular subjects per day, personalizing assignments, or conveying formative feedback—if forgoing homework altogether is not an option. Grading homework misapplies summative grades instead of providing formative assessment. Tying homework to student needs and providing feedback via homework increase achievement instead of stifling motivation because of insurmountable odds.

Reflection Questions

Use the following questions to initiate faculty discussions and assist faculty to examine standards-based grading's potential, which includes separating product, process, and progress criteria, as well as changing the way teachers assign homework.

1. What is the purpose of the homework you assign—practicing skills, learning content, providing feedback, or contributing to student organization and responsibility?

2. How do (or can) your homework assignments provide teacher and student feedback that contributes to content mastery?

3. Historically, high-achieving student grades have tended to be based on a combination of process and product criteria, while low-achieving student grades have tended to be based on process and progress criteria. How can moving to standards-based grading change this trend? What would the consequences be?

4. If students are graded based on process criteria such as attendance, punctuality, and class participation, is it reasonable to expect those skills and behaviors to be taught in ways that allow students to learn and develop them?

5. Researchers such as O'Connor and Wormeli (2011) contend that students learn when teachers let them correct errors and resubmit work and retake tests. However, some teachers, administrators, students, and parents perceive such practices as unfair and contributing to a lack of responsibility. How do you reconcile these opposing views?

Source: O'Connor, K., & Wormeli, R. (2011). Reporting student learning. Educational Leadership, *69(3), 40–44.*

CHAPTER 5

Effectively Address Poverty and Its Variables

Changing from traditional grading practices to standards-based grading is a *major* change for schools. When schools try to make such a change without long-term study and the involvement of multiple stakeholders, retrenchment can occur (Skyward, n.d.). Many practices are embedded in a school's culture and have been for generations. Parents whose children benefit from being rewarded for many of the process factors, such as compliance, often like these practices.

Regardless of the grading practices followed, the task of educating a larger and more diverse school population will be easier for both teachers and students in grades K–12 if schools significantly increase the number of students leaving grade 3 reading proficiently; based on 2015 NAEP scores, less than 40 percent do (NCES, 2015a).

Simply documenting and informing students they have failed is insufficient in standards-based grading, which scaffolds instruction, provides focused feedback, and gives students opportunities to redo assignments. Motivating students—especially those who struggle—to work and rework becomes a critical factor in boosting achievement. Asking them to think differently about their responsibilities is related as well. If students are to learn from failure, failure must be viewed as a temporary delay in mastering content. In this chapter we show how schools can tap into the data related to helping students establish a growth mindset and develop persistence, or what Angela Lee Duckworth calls *grit* (as cited in Perkins-Gough, 2013). If we can accept this thinking, we must examine grading practices that allow students to retake tests or redo work. People do fail in the real world, but those who learn from failure achieve.

As noted previously, poverty is a variable that has far-reaching academic and quality-of-life effects. Poverty's widespread effects challenge educators, and solving these persistent effects is not easy. How are we to reach the young children of families in poverty so as to strengthen their abilities, attitudes, and learning? In this chapter, you'll also find promising strategies for offsetting poverty's drastic effects—programs schools have implemented, plans for early literacy instruction, mentoring via peer tutoring, encouraging a growth mindset, and the gradual release of responsibility.

School Programs

In New York City, a major effort to upgrade academic achievements has resulted in dramatic improvements throughout the Harlem Children's Zone (Chiles, 2013). Schools in the Harlem Children's Zone incorporate music, arts, and sports to engage students. Harlem Children's Zone's specific solutions allow students to operate in realms they're knowledgeable about, which builds their confidence and helps burn off excess energy. The result is that student grade-level performance at the Harlem Children's Zone schools is above 90 percent every year. In addition, almost 100 percent of its students go on to college (Chiles, 2013). Recognizing the needs students have beyond strict academics—reaching past the sort-and-select practice—influences policy and, in cases such as Harlem Children's Zone, leads to greater student achievement and preparation.

In July 2014, President Barack Obama announced that many school districts were joining My Brother's Keeper (www.whitehouse.gov/my-brothers-keeper), an initiative to help struggling students succeed in school (Rich, 2014; The White House, Office of the Press Secretary, 2014). This program does not rely on federal funding but on support from numerous foundations, which together plan to address the widespread and varied needs the Presidential Task Force identifies. The task force identifies six milestones that predict success later in life.

1. Starting school healthy and ready to learn

2. Reading at a third-grade level by third grade

3. Graduating college ready and career ready

4. Furthering education after high school (be it in trade school or college)

5. Entering the workforce prepared

6. Receiving second chances

Educators are aware of and can encourage parents to participate in many of these milestones, including reading by third grade. Some are potentially tougher sells for educators, including second chances. Taking advantage of these initiatives where possible in the classroom is one way to help boost student achievement for low-income students. Making sure to share these resources with parents is another way to help ensure these students get the help they need to eventually become ready for college and careers.

Early Literacy Instruction

Betty Hart and Todd R. Risley's report on the lag in the number of words youth in low-income families are exposed to led to Dana Suskind's creation of the Thirty Million Words™ Initiative (http://thirtymillionwords.org), which is designed to combat the effects of poverty on children's academic success (Suskind, Suskind, & LeWinter-Suskind, 2015). Suskind and colleagues believe this initiative will help students experience greater success in school by contributing to reading comprehension and ultimately reducing failure rates. (Visit **go.SolutionTree.com/instruction** to access live links to the websites mentioned in this book.) Teachers can communicate this initiative and its resources to parents.

Literacy and poverty are directly linked. Students who enter school lacking literacy skills tend to have below-average reading skills in later grades (Hull, 2011). This pattern can lead to broad, long-lasting societal effects such as unemployment, increased crime, and dependency on social welfare (Karoly & Bigelow, 2005). We must double or triple rates of reading growth in grades preK–3 to prevent these longstanding detrimental effects and ensure that our students reach grade level or above performance by the end of third grade. These accelerated rates of growth are required for virtually all students who enter school lacking literacy skills. Acceleration—not retention—is the best evidence-based data we have to support this claim.

Whether or not a student learns to read cannot be left to chance. Most public schools have little or no control over the quality of their students' preschool literacy experiences; therefore, we must focus on the factors we *can* control. For all students to read on or above grade level by the time they complete grade 3, consider doing the following.

- Significantly increase instructional time for literacy and build such time into the master schedule so results can be monitored and evaluated.

- Reflect this increased time in the master schedule to include all aspects of competent literacy program delivery; essentially, for acceleration to make a difference, early literacy groups must receive—at appropriate task and text levels—at least two thirty- to thirty-five-minute, assessment-based, directed instructional groups daily for a minimum of three hundred minutes weekly.

- Use literacy teams to build the collective capacity of teachers to teach reading; create a focus on collaboration so that teachers can work together systematically to analyze and improve their classroom activities ensuring continuous improvements in student literacy learning (DuFour, 2004). Forming such collaborative teams promotes discussions about how best to support and increase student achievement of instructional goals throughout the school year.

- Provide instruction in homogeneous small groups focused on identified skill needs. Use the principles of parallel block scheduling to help reduce literacy groups' size, and help primary teachers by *not* expecting them to manage an entire class while they are instructing the small literacy groups at the same time. Parallel block scheduling has "regular classroom lessons in one block and support services and extension activities in the other. All support activities, including pull-out programs, are scheduled within the parallel block" (Canady, 1988, p. 65). See chapter 6 (page 71) for examples of parallel block scheduling that include blended learning and reduced sizes for instructional groups.

- Provide targeted, intensified instruction in all RTI tiers, with a focus on Tier 1. With RTI, teachers divide instruction into three levels, or tiers. Tier 1 focuses specifically within the core curriculum, with instruction targeting all students. Tier 2 provides additional interventions (usually small-group instruction). Tier 3 interventions, often one-on-one, are provided to students who continue to have difficulties after spending time in Tier 2.

- Establish targets to guide instruction for early readers beginning day one of prekindergarten and kindergarten. Establish a literacy-monitoring management system for each student entering prekindergarten and kindergarten, as well as for any other nonproficient students.

Beyond lobbying for schoolwide schedule changes, teachers can make efforts in their classrooms. While providing instruction, teachers can identify variations in literacy development through simple assessments, such as noticing whether students can identify the alphabet's letters, read and write their own names, read or recognize commercial signs or highway signs, recite nursery rhymes and song lyrics, and name characters from picture books and TV shows. If such informal observations show young students' literacy skills considerably below the norm, teachers can provide additional time and more explicit instruction to those students (Wren, 2000).

All too often, students who enter school with below-average language development face the very real prospect of school failure. One promising solution to this widespread challenge is the CanRead framework, where trained literacy teams "provide intensive small-group literacy instruction that is built into a school's master schedule" (Canady & Canady, 2012). To begin the program, the school identifies a literacy coach from among the faculty; then the literacy coach works with the administrative team, principal, or both to identify and develop the early literacy team, a group of teachers who go from classroom to classroom to provide small-group literacy instruction. At the same time, the literacy coach also works with classroom teachers to identify students who need such accelerated and explicit instruction the most. The early literacy team schedules classroom visits during intervention and enrichment periods and provides assessment-based instruction for small groups of students on such skills as word recognition, fluency, and comprehension. These literacy efforts are crucial to student achievement in the short and long run, and to their quality of life via career and college readiness. Visit **go.SolutionTree.com/instruction** for resources that detail accelerating literacy in the early years.

Mentors and Peer Tutors

Peer tutoring can provide assistance to students who need extra help in academic subjects and also can create a helpful structure for friendly interaction between students (Allen, 2011). In fact, research shows that peer-tutored students achieve more academically and benefit from increased motivation as well as other positive effects (Topping, 2008). Rick Allen (2011) defines various approaches to peer tutoring:

> In cross-age tutoring, older students tutor younger students. In cross-ability tutoring, the student acting as tutor has already attained greater mastery of the subject or material being taught, while the other student might be struggling. In reciprocal tutoring, students of the same age or ability take turns being the tutor.

Peer tutoring offers a clear structure for interactions between tutor and tutee, with specific emphasis aligned with classroom instruction, school or classroom culture, and the varied levels of student motivation. Data show that peer tutoring improves academic achievement while simultaneously improving social and emotional learning—including self-control (Topping, 2008).

Mentoring, especially academically focused mentoring, also can contribute to student achievement. Hawkins, Catalano, and Miller (1992) report that relationships with others and bonds with social institutions, such as schools, can help buffer the effects of stressful life events and promote normal adjustment. Simons-Morton, Crump, Haynie, and Saylor (1999) also report that adolescents who form a positive affiliation or bond with their school are more likely than those without such a bond to engage in prosocial behaviors and to achieve to their academic potential. They also are less likely to engage in anti-social behaviors such as fighting, bullying, truancy, vandalism, and substance use.

Portwood, Ayers, Kinnison, Waris, and Wise (2005) evaluated the effectiveness of one particular school-based mentoring program as a prevention strategy. The mentoring program, entitled Youth Friends, served 170 students across five school districts. Analysis of students' academic performance revealed a positive effect for students who had low grades at baseline.

Growth Mindset

Studies of resilience have become an important source of understanding how school experiences can foster a growth mindset (Werner, 2003). Schools have the opportunity to foster student resilience. Opportunities include, but are not limited to, ongoing development of caring relationships; positive role models and mentors; and clear boundaries and expectations. All the adults in a school can reinforce factors such as reasoning skills and self-control. Teachers also can create structure around routines (Henderson, 2013). According to Henderson (2013), "too often, children who experience abuse, neglect, and other childhood traumas find in their mirrors the message that they are unwanted and unlovable." Wolin and Wolin (1993) conclude that the single most powerful environmental protective factor is one or more caring, believing alternate mirrors. Many children find such a mirror at school—a teacher, counselor, nurse, bus driver, school secretary, or volunteer who communicates, "I see what is right with you, despite your struggles. And I believe what is right with you is more powerful than anything that is wrong."

While children living in urban poverty may face unique challenges, schools are important for building resilience for all students. Many white rural and working-class youth encounter disappointment, struggles, and negative conditions (Deaton, 2013; Putnam, 2015). Vance (2016) has referred to this particular demographic as a "culture in crisis." Standards-based grading includes supports at school which all students, but especially struggling students, need to boost achievement.

Until struggling students experience success in school, educators must provide support structures. Struggling students need a grading system that supports them in redoing work until standards are mastered. They also need process criteria, such as following directions and meeting deadlines, and progress criteria, such as level of student improvement in a specific area, to be separate from product criteria. Once students experience success, they often begin to believe they can be successful in school and then strive for more successful experiences.

Fostering this belief (or *growth mindset*) in students will help them see that they possess intelligence that is developable, not inherent. Students with this mindset "seek challenges, learn from mistakes, and keep faith in themselves in the face of failure" (Sparks, 2013). In other words, such students are optimistic about their personal abilities. On the other hand, failure discourages students who believe in a *fixed mindset,* and they become reluctant to take on more challenges. They become pessimistic about their own potential (Sparks, 2013).

Hearing how other students got their answers can help a class replicate the process: thinking through ideas to arrive at correct answers. This kind of teacher questioning reflects the importance of taking the spotlight off fixed ability and emphasizes the advantages of sharing the learning process—the growth mindset—among students rather than simply praising correct answers from one or two students without describing the problem or explaining the problem-solving process (Sparks, 2013). Sparks cites an example of a ninth-grade student who starts the school year reading at the fifth-grade level, but finishes at the tenth-grade level, largely because his teachers notice his efforts and encourage him to read for thirty minutes on his own time.

Students may respond to frustration and failure by thinking they should just give up, but Dweck's (2014) approach relies on sharing testimonials from other students to show that those negative feelings and beliefs can change, thus strengthening the growth mindset and fostering the development of grit among all students. The growth mindset includes the determination to work hard. Students who must put forth extra effort (and those who grow up in poverty face readiness and literacy lags that require extra efforts) need this sort of determined thinking. One example is described in the epilogue at the end of this book. Standards-based grading is rooted in a growth mindset that students can learn from failure when they receive focused feedback within the context of a supportive environment.

Gradual Release of Responsibility

Refusal to accept a late paper can be viewed as working against a growth mindset and also against a student's development of responsibility. As an example, from Hill and Nave (2009), if a father were to tell his son to clean his room by a certain day and time, but later discover that his son has not met the deadline, would a typical father respond: "Now, son, since you did not clean your room on time, I am *not* going to let you clean your room?" Perhaps consequences and, surely, further encouragement would follow. Perhaps a parent would demonstrate how to make the bed or how to hang up shirts or how to put away games and toys, perhaps making jokes and telling chummy stories throughout the process. At home or at school, modeling is part of the strategy of encouraging student perseverance and eventually becoming responsible. Once students experience success, many students will want to experience additional success and will work toward that end. When this point occurs, the odds are increased that, over time, those students will need fewer supports and less nagging (Canady, n.d.b).

As long as students are working, growing, and improving, grades must follow in order for students to see a purpose in working (Stiggins, 2004, 2007). Perseverance, or what some call *grit*, is developed when students learn that work or effort pays off.

Gradually releasing responsibility to students, often termed *scaffolding*, is another teaching strategy for boosting achievement. This approach provides a specific structure for transitioning classroom instruction from teacher-centered, whole-group instruction to student-centered collaboration and eventual independence. Constance Weaver (2002) suggests the following four action steps for helping students develop independence as readers and writers.

1. The teacher demonstrates reading and writing as he or she reads and brainstorms the text's meaning aloud, talking while writing.

2. The teacher invites the students to participate.

3. Students do the work with help from the teacher when needed. The teacher suggests strategies to support the students and helps them use those strategies.

4. Students use the strategies and skills they've learned to read and write independently, with a partner, or in a small group.

Table 5.1 gives class-level examples of the gradual release of responsibility for learning. Elementary teachers can use this chart as they help students develop into independent readers.

Table 5.1: Gradual Release of Responsibility From Teacher to Students

Action Steps	Classroom Activities
1. The teacher demonstrates reading and writing as he or she reads and brainstorms the text's meaning aloud, talking while writing.	• **Modeled reading:** The teacher or a student does a read-aloud. • **Modeled writing:** The teacher demonstrates for students how to complete a certain type of writing task or how to use a specific writing technique.
2. The teacher invites the students to participate.	• **Shared reading:** The students read or are involved in the book in some way. • **Shared writing:** Students help plan the text and tell the teacher what and how to write. • **Interactive writing:** Students write and the teacher helps, supplying some letters as needed.
3. Students do the work with help from the teacher when needed. The teacher suggests strategies to support the students and helps them use those strategies.	• **Guided reading:** Students read at their own paces while the teacher monitors and provides guided practice. • **Guided writing:** Students write while the teacher monitors and provides guided practice.
4. Students use the strategies and skills they've learned to read and write independently, with a partner, or in a small group.	• **Sustained reading:** Students read on their own or with a peer or small group; the teacher tends not to offer reading assistance. • **Sustained writing:** Students write on their own or with a peer or small group; the teacher tends not to offer writing assistance.

Source: Adapted from Weaver, 2002.

Fisher and Frey (2007) propose a more general plan focusing on helping students develop process skills such as organizing notes, meeting deadlines, and following rules. Sometimes referred to as *I do it, we do it, you do it*, the plan includes demonstration, prompt, and practice. Ellen Levy (2007) further developed Fisher and Frey's (2007) plan by defining the specific stages in greater detail by describing teacher and student roles and responsibilities in developing student independence.

See table 5.2 (page 68) for the gradual release of responsibility and student and teacher roles and responsibilities. Student independence is a likely outcome when teachers provide support and then gradually reduce it in the manners suggested.

Table 5.2: Mentoring Roles and Responsibilities

	Levels of Teacher Support	Teacher Roles and Responsibilities	Student Roles and Responsibilities
I do it	Highest level of support; direct instruction	• Provides direct instruction • Establishes goals and purpose • Models • Thinks aloud	• Actively listens • Takes notes • Asks for clarification
We do it	Guided instruction	• Provides interactive instruction • Works with students • Checks, prompts, and provides clues • Provides additional modeling • Meets with needs-based groups	• Asks and responds to questions • Works with teacher and classmates • Completes process alongside others
You do it together	Guided instruction	• Moves among groups • Clarifies confusion • Provides support	• Works with classmates and shares outcome • Collaborates on authentic task • Consolidates learning • Completes process in small group • Looks to peers for clarification
You do it independently	Lowest level of support or no support	• Provides feedback • Evaluates student progress • Determines level of understanding	• Works alone • Relies on notes and classroom activities • Takes full responsibility for outcome

Source: Adapted from Fisher & Frey, 2007.

Summary

Rethinking grading practices and evaluating instructional support are especially crucial. Poverty, linked to so many academic disadvantages, including low literacy, is something that teachers can address in their classrooms and with parents. Motivation and achievement increase when students are taught that their minds are malleable, when peers help them learn, and when they gradually develop more responsibility for their education. Teachers can approach grades differently to add these positive effects.

Reflection Questions

Use the following questions to help initiate faculty discussions and assist faculty to examine the potential of implementing programs that offset poverty's negative academic effects on students.

1. For any student, but particularly students living in poverty, one of the most important school functions is becoming a proficient reader by the end of grade 3. What research-based strategies can you initiate at your school or district to help low-achieving students achieve at accelerated rates in the early grades?

2. How can you offer mentoring and peer tutoring to provide support for low-achieving students in your school or district?

3. How do the following teacher-to-student communications facilitate a growth mindset?

   • "Your writing project was well organized, but you need to add descriptive language. Review yesterday's notes and add descriptive language in the places marked."

   • "Great job! Be prepared to share in class today how you were able to solve the problem correctly."

   • "You kept working on your project until you got it right. Congratulations!"

   • "I recommended you for a tutoring session during your intervention and enrichment period beginning tomorrow at 11 am. Bring your last test, and a tutor will help you prepare for reassessment."

4. How can the *I do it, we do it, you do it* language (Fisher & Frey, 2007) help teachers foster student responsibility for their own learning? What challenges does this model present with implementation?

Source: Fisher, D., & Frey, N. (2007). Implementing a schoolwide literacy framework: Improving achievement in an urban elementary school. The Reading Teacher, 61(32–45). Accessed at www .sjboces.org/doc/Gifted/GradualReleaseResponsibilityJan08.pdf on November 21, 2016.

CHAPTER 6

Rethink Scheduling

The person who designs the master schedule has power! There are many ways the designer, typically one of the school's administrators with help from a leadership team, can build the master schedule to help boost student achievement. A schedule design has ripple effects. The following components have consequences, for example.

- **Class length:** The number of minutes in a class period is a factor in determining how many classes meet in a school day, and that factor is related to how many movements students make in a school day. Student movements influence school management, such as the number of reported tardies and disciplinary referrals.

- **Teaching strategies:** The number of minutes in a class period is a factor in determining teaching strategies for utilization on a large scale, such as employing project-based learning, using technology, completing writing assignments, conducting Socratic seminars, and providing student support. Teaching strategies that involve in-depth learning and relevancy help explain retention theory.

- **Teacher workload:** The number of minutes in a class period is a factor in determining teacher workload; the total number of students assigned to a teacher at any one time period is a factor in determining whether teachers regularly perform the most productive teaching functions—for instance, making it difficult for students to fail or to get a good grade without work and rework, providing focused feedback, and grading in pencil as long as possible (Ouchi, 2009).

- **Student workload:** The number of minutes in the class period is typically related to student workloads. For example, students enrolled in four classes at one time (versus eight classes) have fewer different homework assignments at any one time, fewer texts and materials to transport, fewer projects and assignments to manage, and fewer classes to fail. In semester block schedules, careful guidance can provide students who lack high motivation and organizational skills two core classes each semester, along with two electives (which tend to have less homework). Students' chances of being successful in schedules with a balanced workload increase when students also receive services that give them the benefits such schedules can offer. A *balanced workload* relates to the number of classes and homework assignments a student is responsible for at any one time period during the school year. For teachers, it is the number of students for whom they are responsible at any one time period (Ouchi, 2009).

- **Instructional minutes:** The number of minutes in class periods is related to the actual number of instructional minutes in the school day (versus clock minutes). Band, physical education, technology, and science lab classes require a certain number of minutes for preparation regardless of class period length; for example, dressing for physical education classes takes the same amount of time if the class is forty-five minutes or eighty minutes; therefore, it is likely that more physical activity occurs in a class that meets every other day for eighty minutes than in a class that meets daily for forty-five minutes. Other administrative routines, such as checking attendance, converting hallway behavior into classroom behavior, and crafting assignments, consume class time and are not directly related to instruction. Quality instructional time and student engaged activities are factors associated with boosting student achievement.

These components all influence the master schedule. In the next section, we'll discuss this scheduling, which includes using strategies that support student achievement.

The Master Schedule

School administrators can build master schedules that support students and assist teachers in their efforts to increase student achievement. Rettig and Canady (2000) provide examples of institutionalizing such support by incorporating I/E (intervention and enrichment) periods and following the EEE (extended time, elective class, or enrichment time) model:

- E = Extended time for some students, such as (1) completing homework, (2) working in computer lab, (3) re-taking tests, advising, counseling, receiving tutoring on specific skills identified from formative assessments, etc.

- E = Elective class for students experiencing few academic difficulties.

- E = Enrichment and additional exploratory opportunities for those temporarily not needing assistance provided during extended time.

The following six time-altering scheduling strategies can provide additional student support during middle and high school hours.

1. **Scheduling pre-electives:** When assessments *for* learning indicate large gaps in skills needed for students to succeed in a required course, schedule pre-electives. Just extending time in a course may not increase achievement. By providing appropriate pre-electives, students obtain needed foundational skills that prevent future failures in required sequenced courses that follow. The Southern Regional Education Board (www.sreb.org) has examples of pre-elective courses that prepare students for high school and college literacy and mathematics.

2. **Building parallel support in a student's schedule:** For example, some students' assessment results may indicate the need to be enrolled in a grade-level mathematics course that meets daily, but simultaneously enrolled for a temporary time in a class period, such as an intervention and enrichment period, for additional support, tutoring, or computer-assisted instruction. Scheduling parallel support also can be helpful for students who are transferring in during the school year and whose personal assessments indicate learning gaps.

3. **Scheduling trailer courses:** Schedule trailer courses for students who marginally pass a sequence-based, foundation-building course, such as algebra 1, English 9, or grade 9 science. A *trailer course* follows a foundational course, and the content must be focused on assessment based on individual student deficits. It is not simply a repeat of the course. Students needing trailer courses tend to be students who receive grades of low Cs and all forms of Ds. Schools offering the four-by-four or semester/semester block schedules can schedule a foundation class during the fall semester, and students who receive Fs can repeat the course during the spring semester, possibly with a tutorial during

a parallel support period. Those who receive grades between a C and D– can be scheduled for a trailer course in the spring that assesses each student's lack of mastery; they focus just on those standards needing additional work. Trailer courses must be personalized and data driven—*not* just reteaching course content. If schools implement standards-based grading, students would not be given a low final grade as described. Instead, they would likely be given an E, extended time grade, and students would continue working on mastering course standards during the following semester.

4. **Pairing selected students with an advisor-tutor:** This person serves as a strong advocate, and, when needed, as a personal tutor to the student needing support. Students who need such support typically have a history of poor attendance and tend to make grades inconsistent with their past performance or their assessed abilities. These students often have little or no support outside of school. The advisor-tutor (peer tutoring is championed as an achievement raiser in chapter 5 on page 59) may not be the one who actually tutors when needed, but will see that the service is provided, perhaps by an older student who can tutor in a particular course. Hill asserts that "Many students would rather get extra help from the student workforce than their teachers" (2014, p. 106). The advocate-tutor's focus is to be constantly monitoring the students who fall below the radar in many schools. Hill (2014) describes this advocate as a *lifeguard*.

5. **Scheduling most IEP students for a preteaching, co-teaching, or reteaching cycle of instruction:** An intervention and enrichment period should be included in master school schedules following this recommended format for IEP students. Controlled heterogeneous groupings also facilitate this cycle of instruction (Canady & Rettig, 2008; Rettig & Canady, 2000).

6. **Scheduling interventions throughout a course:** *High-sequence* courses, such as mathematics, which build on foundational courses, are particularly notorious for compounding a struggling student's difficulties. For example, a student who does not understand a mathematics concept that is taught in the fall will continue to struggle throughout the academic year if he or she doesn't receive intervention throughout a course. It is very difficult for teachers working alone to provide interventions throughout a course. Where interventions are provided on a long-term basis, teachers work in pairs or in teams and develop block schedules where interventions can occur every ten,

fifteen, or twenty-two days. The cycles provided are possibilities; no one cycle is superior to another. See Rettig and Canady (1998, 2000) for schedules built for mathematics teams and teacher pairings.

School personnel who have implemented standards-based grading find it easier to implement these student support structures; in fact, standards-based grading, when implemented with fidelity, requires that similar structures be in place. See figure 6.1, which shows how *vertical enrichment* occurs when students move beyond age and grade level (for example, a sixth grader moving to seventh- and eighth-grade mathematics materials). *Horizontal enrichment* occurs when students experience deeper instruction at the level they are currently working.

TEACH

Determine essential standards that *must* be mastered.

Provide collaborative lesson planning.

Offer pre-electives for selected students, based on assessments *for* learning.

Schedule parallel support for selected students.

Provide sustained interventions for high-sequenced courses.

Schedule a preteach, co-teach, reteach cycle of instruction for IEP students.

ACT

Identify students who mastered, partially mastered, and did not master and must be retaught.

Schedule trailer courses for partially mastered standards.

Scaffold and differentiate instruction for students needing reteaching.

Reteach with support, such as scheduling an advisor-tutor, parallel support, or both for students needing reteaching.

Complete reteaching cycle; reassess and determine next action steps.

Schedule extended learning with vertical enrichment, horizontal enrichment, or both for those who demonstrated mastery.

ASSESS

Align all assessments to summative assessments.

Determine levels of mastery: mastered, partially mastered, and little or no mastery.

ANALYZE

Review assessment results with PLC members.

Diagnose and look for gaps in student learning.

Determine implications for instruction.

© 2016 Jennifer Kent. Used with permission.

Figure 6.1: Standards-based instructional cycle with suggested scheduling supports.

It is important to note that just changing a schedule, such as providing small groups, does not guarantee a boost in student achievement. However, a schedule can be a catalyst that facilitates the changes that do boost student achievement, such as preassessing, providing focused feedback, insisting students redo work, reteaching, reassessing, and grading in pencil as long as possible. So an instructional change in the schedule, like providing small groups, *can* have a huge impact. For example, students of lower socioeconomic status and minority students receive greater benefits from smaller classes than their more affluent peers (Finn & Achilles, 1990). Based on Biddle and Berliner's (2002) research, Canady and Rettig (2008) summarize a major benefit of small classes for students: "Students whose classes are small in the early grades retain their gains in standard size classrooms and in the upper grades, middle school and high school" (pp. 147–148).

The remainder of this chapter illustrates multiple types of schedules for elementary, middle, and high schools. We also describe alternative school schedules. All the schedules have various types of student supports included, which are needed if standards-based grading is implemented with fidelity. Several of the models provide teachers time to work with both whole groups and small groups throughout the day. Small groups are critical for teachers in the primary grades because they must have flexible, skill-based groups of four to six students until the students become strong beginning readers. At that point, groups of six to ten are acceptable (Walpole & McKenna, 2016).

Elementary School

During intervention and enrichment periods, elementary students who still need intervention in basic reading and mathematics skills can receive additional instruction, practice, or both, while those who have attained proficiency in literacy and mathematics can receive enrichment. Simply extending academic course time for students does not necessarily result in significant achievement gains. Additional course time is more likely to produce positive results when the extended time is focused, intentional, assessment based, and personal (Farbman, Goldberg, & Miller, 2014). Our elementary school sample schedules incorporate various instructional tiers with the focus of accelerating literacy achievement during the primary grades. If we expect to improve achievement for a wide spectrum of students, we need elementary school schedules that provide teachers with ways to work with small literacy groups without having students spend so much time working independently in centers and teachers having to teach small groups and manage the remaining students simultaneously.

Accelerating literacy rates in the early grades is crucial for increasing the number of college- or career-ready graduates. Successful reading acceleration requires that educators provide extended time for literacy with varying size groupings based on students' needs and strategically differentiated instruction across *whole groups* and *reduced groups*, as the schedules in this chapter illustrate. Figure 6.2 (page 78) is a sample master schedule with literacy blocks and early literacy groups built into the master schedule—along with intervention and enrichment periods for grades 2–5. Literacy Team 1 works with students in kindergarten and grade 1. As you study the schedule, note that if the school can staff a second literacy team, Literacy Team 2 works with students in prekindergarten, grade 2, and students in grade 3 who still need support. The instruction for grade 3 can occur during the third-grade intervention and enrichment period. Early literacy groups for grades 2 and 3 should serve a limited number of students who have been in the school and also serve transfer students who recently entered the school. Visit **go.SolutionTree.com/instruction** to read research that builds a case for accelerating literacy in early grades.

Grade 3 students who still need early literacy groups are often transfer students who have missed the early literacy skills taught in grades K–2. The second literacy team also teaches during grades 3–5 intervention and enrichment periods. The afternoon early literacy group blocks for grades preK–1 (period VI) overlap to accommodate cross-grade-level groupings, which may be needed as the school year progresses.

Grades 2 and 3, as well as grades 4 and 5, have three equal blocks scheduled; these parallel blocks are helpful if teachers in these grades wish to departmentalize or cross grade levels for skill groups or for sharing staff. Periods are forty to fifty minutes, depending on the number of minutes in the school day. Lunch periods may need to be adjusted, depending on when the school day begins, the number of students in the school, and the number of seats in the cafeteria.

Grade 1

Figure 6.3 (page 79) illustrates how the principles of parallel block scheduling can be combined with technology to provide three first-grade teachers whole-group time and then reduced-group time, without their having to manage the remaining students in seatwork or centers. Based on experience working with schools, when teachers don't have to manage the remainder of the classroom, it is easier to keep students' attention in small groups and to spend more time teaching them. In this elementary school schedule, the reduced-group time is repeated twice daily; and a support person, as figure 6.3 indicates with a checkmark (✓), comes in to co-teach with the regular teacher so that group size for all emergent readers is between four and six students. These groups' small size is an instructional standard to maintain until the students become beginning readers; then you can provide groups of six to ten students. In addition to using principles of parallel block scheduling to provide reduced groupings, your

	I	II	III	IV	V	VI	VII	VIII	IX
Prekindergarten	Early literacy groups		Early literacy groups	Early literacy groups	Recess and lunch	Early literacy groups	Early literacy groups	Early literacy groups ↕	
Kindergarten	Early literacy groups		Early literacy groups	Early literacy groups	Recess and lunch	Early literacy groups ↕	Encore/plan	Repeat a.m. early literacy groups	
Grade 1	Early literacy groups		Mathematics and science	Mathematics and science	Recess and lunch	Repeat a.m. early literacy groups ↕		Encore/plan	Social studies
Grade 2	Literacy ↕		Literacy and social studies ↕	Literacy and social studies	Intervention and enrichment	Recess and lunch	Mathematics and science ↕	Mathematics and science	Encore/plan
Grade 3	Literacy ↕		Literacy and social studies	Literacy and social studies	Encore/plan	Recess and lunch	Mathematics and science		Intervention and enrichment
Grade 4			Intervention and enrichment	Encore/plan			Lunch and recess		
Grade 5			**Encore/plan	Intervention and enrichment		↕	Recess and lunch		
Lunch and recess					Prekindergarten, kindergarten, grade 1	Grades 2, 3	Grades 4, 5		
Encore/plan	*Plan		Grade 5	Grade 4	Grade 3	Lunch	Kindergarten	Grade 1	Grade 2
Literacy team 1	Grade 1		Kindergarten			Grade 1		Kindergarten	
Literacy team 2	Prekindergarten and grade 2		Intervention and enrichment 4	Intervention and enrichment 5	Lunch	Prekindergarten and kindergarten	Prekindergarten and grade 1	Prekindergarten and kindergarten	Intervention and enrichment 3
Intervention and enrichment			Grade 4	Grade 5	Grade 2	Lunch			Grade 3

*Available to provide seventy-five to ninety minutes of extended plan time on a six- or twelve-school-day rotation. (See Canady and Rettig, 2008, pp. 83–92, for more details in scheduling extended planning time.)

**Encore refers to classes such as art, music, physical education, media, and dance. It is during these class periods that groups of teachers have common planning time.

↕ indicates how groupings and staffing can occur easily across grade levels.

Figure 6.2: Sample elementary school master schedule.

Teachers	Period X	Period Y	Period Z
Teacher A	Whole groups 1 and 4	Reduced group 1 ✓	Reduced group 4 ✓
Teacher B	Reduced group 5 ✓	Whole groups 2 and 5	Reduced group 2 ✓
Teacher C	Reduced group 3 ✓	Reduced group 6 ✓	Whole groups 3 and 6
Extension staff: • Title I teacher • RTI resource • Special education teacher • Talented and gifted teacher • English learner teacher • Teacher's aide • Reading specialist • Computer lab technician	Whole groups 2 and 6	Whole groups 3 and 4	Whole groups 1 and 5

✓ = A support teacher such as Title I, RTI resource, English language, or special education teacher serves as a co-teacher with the reduced groups.

Figure 6.3: Three-period parallel block schedule for grade 1.

school might use the principles of controlled heterogeneous groupings to determine the initial groupings. *Controlled heterogeneous grouping* reduces the range of student needs within an instructional class, which allows teachers to better address the group's needs (Canady & Rettig, 2008; Rettig & Canady, 2000). After the first nine weeks of the school year, the support person represented in figure 6.3 probably will be pulled from reduced groups 5 and 6 because those students are likely to have moved beyond the beginning reader stage. The support person then moves to grades 2 and 3 to assist transfer students who need support similar to emergent readers.

In the sample schedule, periods X, Y, and Z can be any three periods in the master schedule; however, it is best if at least two of the periods are back to back. Periods should be at least thirty to forty minutes, depending on the length of the school day. This three-way parallel block should be scheduled twice daily, which requires a minimum of two ninety or two one-hundred–minute blocks of time in the master schedule.

Most of the literacy support teachers in this example are special education teachers or teachers' aides whom the literacy coach has trained in primary literacy instruction (Walpole & McKenna, 2013). The school in this example has a large IEP population so it uses more than 12 percent of its special education budget to improve Tier 1 literacy instruction for all students in an attempt to reduce the number of students who might eventually need Tier 2 and Tier 3 services. The teachers know that until Tier 1 literacy instruction is improved, the school will continue to spend unequal portions of its regular budget on Tier 2 and Tier 3 services. A special education aide operates the computers for several of the grade levels.

Grades 2 and 3

Figure 6.4 illustrates how two teachers in grade 2 and two teachers in grade 3 share the same blocks of time and the same extension staff, but do not have to mix the groups. In this example, periods W, X, Y, and Z can be any four periods in the master schedule; however, it is best if at least two of the periods are together. Periods should be at least thirty to forty minutes, and the blocks of time should be scheduled twice daily and embedded in the master schedule. This type of schedule provides elementary teachers with time to work with small groups without having to develop and supervise activities for other students.

Teachers	Period W	Period X	Period Y	Period Z
Teacher A: Grade 2	Whole groups 1 and 3		Reduced group 1 ✓	Reduced group 3
Teacher B: Grade 2	Whole groups 2 and 4		Reduced group 4	Reduced group 2 ✓
Teacher C: Grade 3	Reduced group 5 ✓	Reduced group 7	Whole groups 5 and 7	
Teacher D: Grade 3	Reduced group 8	Reduced group 6 ✓	Whole groups 6 and 8	
Extension staff: • Title I teacher • Special education teacher • Talented and gifted teacher • English learner teacher • Teacher's aide • Reading specialist • Computer lab technician	Whole groups 6 and 7	Whole groups 5 and 8	Whole groups 2 and 3	Whole groups 1 and 4

✓ = A support teacher such as Title I, RTI resource, English language, or special education teacher serves as a co-teacher with the reduced groups.

Figure 6.4: Four-period parallel block schedule for grades 2 and 3.

The following elementary sample schedules create reduced groups for three periods a day.

Grades 4 and 5

Figure 6.5 and figure 6.6 (page 82) illustrate how elementary master schedules can be designed to provide teachers with reduced groups for three periods a day without having to manage other students in the classroom. Again, the principles of parallel block scheduling are employed in these schedules. In these schedules, three teachers have been assigned to grade 4 and three to grade 5; three teachers teach the reading, language arts, and social studies content to both grades, which figure 6.5 illustrates, and three teachers teach the mathematics and science block to both grades, which figure 6.6 shows.

Teachers	Period X	Period Y	Period Z
Teacher A Reading, language arts, and social studies	Whole groups 1 and 4	Reduced group 1 ✓	Reduced group 4 ✓
Teacher B Reading, language arts, and social studies	Reduced group 5 ✓	Whole groups 2 and 5	Reduced group 2 ✓
Teacher C Reading, language arts, and social studies	Reduced group 3 ✓	Reduced group 6 ✓	Whole groups 3 and 6
Extension staff: • Title I teacher • Special education teacher • Talented and gifted teacher • English learner teacher • Teacher's aide • Reading specialists • Computer lab technician	Whole groups 2 and 6	Whole groups 3 and 4	Whole groups 1 and 5

✓ = A support teacher such as Title I, RTI resource, English language, or special education teacher serves as a co-teacher with the reduced groups.

Figure 6.5: Three-period parallel block schedule for reading, language arts, and social studies in grades 4 and 5.

Figure 6.5 presents a schedule for instruction in fourth- and fifth-grade reading, language arts, and social studies. Periods X, Y, and Z can be any three periods in the master schedule; however, it is best if at least two of the periods are together. At these grade levels, periods should be between thirty-five to forty-five minutes, depending on the number of minutes in the school day. The reading,

Teachers	Period X	Period Y	Period Z
Teacher A Mathematics and science	Whole groups 1 and 4	Reduced group 1 ✓	Reduced group 4 ✓
Teacher B Mathematics and science	Reduced group 5 ✓	Whole groups 2 and 5	Reduced group 2 ✓
Teacher C Mathematics and science	Reduced group 3 ✓	Reduced group 6 ✓	Whole groups 3 and 6
Extension staff: • Title I reading teacher • Special education teacher • Talented and gifted teacher • English learner teacher • Teacher's aide • Reading specialists • Computer lab technician	Whole groups 2 and 6	Whole groups 3 and 4	Whole groups 1 and 5

✓ = A support teacher such as Title I, RTI resource, English language, or special education teacher serves as a co-teacher with the reduced groups.

Figure 6.6: Three-period parallel block schedule for mathematics and science in grades 4 and 5.

language arts, and social studies team works three periods opposite the mathematics and science team. When one team is working with students in grade 4, the other team is working with students in grade 5.

Figure 6.6 illustrates a parallel block schedule where three teachers teach mathematics and science. In one of the three periods, they have whole groups composed of their two reduced groups. This plan allows instruction to the whole group, while the small groups provide time for skills and support. Some days, the whole group can be used for basic mathematics and science instruction, while the small groups will allow for personal assistance when needed.

Because the quality of the teacher is a critical school variable in student achievement, in this schedule teams are based on the teachers' strongest skills. While one team teaches grade 4 students, the other team instructs students in grade 5; and then the teams reverse groupings during the day. The morning and afternoon blocks are rotated every nine weeks.

The figure illustrates the mathematics and science schedule. Periods X, Y, and Z can be any three periods in the master schedule; however, it is best if at least two of the periods are together. At these grade levels, periods should be between thirty-five to forty-five minutes, depending on the number of minutes in the school day. The reading, language arts, and social studies team works three periods opposite the mathematics and science team. When one team is working with students in grade 4, the other team is working with students in grade 5.

Parallel block scheduling provides teachers structured time to deliver students whole-group and reduced-group instruction primarily in reading and mathematics. The extension time also gives support teachers opportunities to work with students with various types of IEPs without pulling them from the core teacher's instructional time. Also, by giving core teachers reduced groups two, three, or four times daily, core teachers can provide more personalized instruction without having to simultaneously manage other students in the classroom. Personalized instruction via small group is highly associated with boosting student achievement (Keefe & Jenkins, 2002).

Concept/Progress Model for Teaching Mathematics in Grades 3–6

Figure 6.7 (page 84) illustrates a concept, or mastery, model for teaching mathematics. This model is based on the principles of parallel block scheduling and controlled heterogeneous groupings. In the schedule, a concept group equals two controlled heterogeneous groups (such as one and four). A progress group equals one performance-based group (five, for example), and it is subject to change based on mastery of standards.

Controlled heterogeneous groups reduce the range of skill needs in a classroom when students are assigned randomly to a class. Teachers can focus specifically on student needs when they schedule whole-group instruction and then reduced-group instruction. This kind of schedule reduces teachers' chance of teaching to the middle and expecting someone to remove the students at the lower end of the achievement range, with students in the upper range stagnating or having to spend much time working independently. In this example, teachers A, B, and C could represent three teachers at individual grades 3–6 in a large elementary school or a mathematics team that serves students at three or four grade levels during different blocks of time designated in the master schedule. This same schedule format can be used for teaching mathematics in middle schools.

Note that in the mathematics block figure 6.7 illustrates, the special education co-teacher (whose specialization can vary) in the mathematics groups (✓) meets with all client groups daily during the school's intervention and enrichment period and

Instructors	SCHOOL DAYS					
	One	**Two**	**Three**	**Four**	**Five**	**Six**
Teacher A	Whole groups 1 and 4	Whole groups 1 and 4	Reduced group 1 ✓	Reduced group 4	Reduced group 1 ✓	Reduced group 4
Teacher B	Reduced group 5	Reduced group 2 ✓	Whole groups 2 and 5	Whole groups 2 and 5	Reduced group 5	Reduced group 2 ✓
Teacher C	Reduced group 3 ✓	Reduced group 6	Reduced group 6	Reduced group 3 ✓	Whole groups 3 and 6	Whole groups 3 and 6
Computer lab or computer carts	Reduced groups 2 and 6	Reduced groups 3 and 5	Reduced groups 3 and 4	Reduced groups 1 and 6	Reduced groups 2 and 4	Reduced groups 1 and 5

✓ = Co-teaching (for example, with special education, English language, Title I, accelerated literacy, or RTI teachers)

Figure 6.7: Sample schedule for grades 3–6.

preteaches the concepts that those students will learn a few days later when joining the other groups. Then the special education support teacher (✓) co-teaches during the reduced-group periods. Following co-teaching, the co-teacher (✓) reteaches during the next day's intervention and enrichment period. This cycle of preteaching, co-teaching, and then reteaching keeps IEP students in the regular curriculum, and with supports it increases their odds of mastering the full curriculum on which they will be tested. This plan also stigmatizes students less.

Middle School

To address the critical need to improve literacy attainment at all school levels, middle school faculties can consider schedules that reduce the workload for students and teachers while also reducing failing time. The following section details sample middle school schedules designed to provide longer class periods and built-in time for students needing additional support. All middle school students can benefit from student-engaged activities, such as project-based learning, if they focus on particular subjects for extended periods of time, which these schedules provide.

Figure 6.8 (pages 86–87) shows a sample middle school schedule where small teams work together; it has nine periods with reading and language arts and mathematics blocked and an EEE period. This schedule also may fit middle schools with low enrollments (or possibly K–8 schools) or schools with limited budgets since it has just one period for electives and teacher planning. The EEE period will allow a time period for elective and exploratory classes for students not requiring interventions and support in core classes. As discussed, EEE stands for extended time, elective, or enrichment time. This type of schedule provides structured support for various student groups; it also facilitates personalized instruction (Keefe & Jenkins, 2002).

Figure 6.9 (pages 88–89) illustrates a middle school schedule for grades 6–8; the schedule has ten periods with reading and language arts and mathematics blocked and an EEE period. You'll notice that sixth-grade core teachers teach two groups of students all year. Ouchi (2009) documents that if teachers are expected to perform the most productive teaching functions, such as providing students with focused feedback and supporting them in doing work over until it is mastered, then the school's scheduling team must provide teachers with schedules that consider the number of students a teacher is assigned during any one period of time (Ouchi, 2009). The *number of students* a teacher instructs during any one period of time seems to be more critical than the *number of periods* a teacher teaches. Therefore, the sample middle school schedule in figure 6.9 illustrates a two-teacher pairing model for grade 6; each pair is composed of one teacher for reading, language arts, and social studies plus one teacher for mathematics and science. For grades 7 and 8, the middle school schedule shows a three-group model (reading and language arts) and (mathematics), with variations for science and social studies. The core teachers can teach three groups at any one time. The loops in the schedules for grades 7 and 8 indicate that science and social studies classes can meet in daily single periods or in rotational blocks, such as day one/day two (A/B) or one quarter on, one quarter off. If the grading period is nine weeks, one teacher can teach science for four and a half weeks while another teaches social studies for that time. After that, the teachers switch classes and repeat lessons. Some teachers prefer units, which tend to be designed for teaching fifteen to eighteen days. Teachers switch classes and repeat units.

For those students whose below-average literacy skills are still a major factor when they enter high school, educators can prepare alternative schedules to support and assist them in attaining at least functional literacy skills before graduating from high school. It is all too clear that students who leave school without diplomas, or with diplomas that do not equip them for college or careers, often remain unemployed; and even when they find work, the jobs are typically at the low end of the wage scale.

GRADE 6A

Grade 6A Teachers and Subjects	Period One	Period Two	Period Three	Period Four	Period Five	Period Six	Period Seven	Period Eight	Period Nine
6A (Reading and language arts)	A	A	B	B	Lunch	EEE	C	C	*Encore/plan
6B (Mathematics)	C	C	A	A	Lunch	EEE	B	B	B
6C (Science and social studies)	B	B	C	C	Lunch	EEE	A	A	A

GRADE 6B

Grade 6B Teachers and Subjects	Period One	Period Two	Period Three	Period Four	Period Five	Period Six	Period Seven	Period Eight	Period Nine
6A (Reading and language arts)	A	A	B	B	Lunch	EEE	C	C	C
6B (Mathematics)	C	C	A	A	Lunch	EEE	B	Encore/plan	B
6C (Science and social studies)	B	B	C	C	Lunch	EEE	A	A	A

GRADE 7A

Grade 7A Teachers and Subjects	Period One	Period Two	Period Three	Period Four	Period Five	Period Six	Period Seven	Period Eight	Period Nine
7A (Reading and language arts)	A	A	B	B	EEE	Lunch	C	C	C
7B (Mathematics)	C	C	A	A	EEE	Lunch	Encore/plan	B	B
7C (Science and social studies)	B	B	C	C	EEE	Lunch	A	A	A

*Encore is for students. Plan is for teachers.

**For grade 6, in the schedule showing one teacher for science and social studies, those two teachers work on both teams. For example, one is teaching science to the 6A team; the social studies teacher is teaching the 6B team. On a rotational basis, they switch teams and repeat units.

GRADE 7B

Grade 7B Teachers and Subjects	Period One	Period Two	Period Three	Period Four	Period Five	Period Six	Period Seven	Period Eight	Period Nine
7A (Reading and language arts)	A	A	B		EEE	Lunch	B	C	C
7B (Mathematics)	C	C	A	*Encore/plan			A	B	B
7C (Science and social studies)	B	B	C				C	A	A

GRADE 8A

Grade 8A Teachers and Subjects	Period One	Period Two	Period Three	Period Four	Period Five	Period Six	Period Seven	Period Eight	Period Nine
8A (Reading and language arts)	A	A	Encore/plan	B	B	EEE	Lunch	C	C
8B (Mathematics)	C	C		A	A			B	B
8C (Science and social studies)	B	B		C	C			A	A

GRADE 8B

Grade 8B Teachers and Subjects	Period One	Period Two	Period Three	Period Four	Period Five	Period Six	Period Seven	Period Eight	Period Nine
8A (Reading and language arts)	Encore/plan	A	A	B	B	EEE	Lunch	C	C
8B (Mathematics)		C	C	A	A			B	B
8C (Science and social studies)		B	B	C	C			A	A

*Encore is for students. Plan is for teachers.

Figure 6.8: Sample middle school schedule with nine periods and EEE time.

Visit go.SolutionTree.com/instruction to download this free reproducible.

GRADE 6

Grade 6 Teachers and Subjects	Period One	Period Two	Period Three	Period Four	Period Five	Period Six	Period Seven	Period Eight	Period Nine	Period Ten
6A (Reading, language arts, and social studies)	A	A	A	Lunch	EEE	D	D	D	Exploratory and physical education	
6B (Reading, language arts, and social studies)	B	B	B			E	E	E		
6C (Reading, language arts, and social studies)	C	C	C			F	F	F		
6D (Mathematics and science)	D	D	D			A	A	A		
6E (Mathematics and science)	E	E	E			B	B	B		
6F (Mathematics and science)	F	F	F			C	C	C		

GRADE 7

Grade 7 Teachers and Subjects	Period One	Period Two	Period Three	Period Four	Period Five	Period Six	Period Seven	Period Eight	Period Nine	Period Ten
7A (Reading and language arts)	A	A	E	E	Lunch	EEE	Exploratory and physical education		C	C
7B (Reading and language arts)	D	D	F	F					B	B
7C (Mathematics)	C	C	A	A					E	E
7D (Mathematics)	B	B	D	D					F	F
7E (Science)	E	F	C	B					A	D
7F (Social studies)	F	E	B	C					D	A

Grade 6 illustrates a two-teacher pairing model. Each pair is composed of one teacher for reading, language arts, and social studies, and one teacher for mathematics and science.

GRADE 8										
Grade 8 Teachers and Subjects	Period One	Period Two	Period Three	Period Four	Period Five	Period Six	Period Seven	Period Eight	Period Nine	Period Ten
8A (Reading, language arts)	A	A	Exploratory and physical education	Exploratory and physical education	EEE	Lunch	C	C	E	E
8B (Reading, language arts)	D	D					B	B	F	F
8C (Mathematics)	C	C					E	E	A	A
8D (Mathematics)	B	B					F	F	D	D
8E (Science)	E	F					A	D	C	B
8F (Social studies)	F	E					D	A	B	C

Grades 7 and 8 allow science and social studies to meet daily, in single periods, or in rotational blocks, such as day 1/day 2 (A/B) or quarter on and quarter off.

Figure 6.9: Sample middle school schedule with ten periods and EEE time.

High School

Those who develop high school schedules should realize that *all* students do not have to follow the *same* schedule if high schools are to develop data-driven student schedules based on student needs. From there, the scheduling team can combine various periods of time to meet the seat time requirements of a year's work and, therefore, qualify students for full credit.

- A minimum of forty minutes of class time meeting daily for 180 school days, divided by sixty minutes, equals 120 clock hours (A few states require only 108 total clock minutes for a year's credit; the provision of 108 total minutes allows single periods of only 36 minutes, *not* 40 minutes of class time.)

- A minimum of eighty minutes of class time meeting daily for ninety days, divided by sixty minutes, equals 120 clock hours

- A minimum of 160 minutes of class time meeting daily for forty-five days, divided by sixty minutes, equals 120 clock hours

- A minimum of 240 minutes of class time meeting daily for thirty days, divided by sixty clock minutes, equals 120 clock hours

Figure 6.10 illustrates these options and offers two versions of intensive schedules for students who enter grade 9 with very low academic skills in literacy and mathematics, the foundational skills necessary to succeed in their other required core classes.

This schedule provides grade 9 students *three years of literacy* and *three years of mathematics instruction* during *one calendar year*. The students also have an opportunity to complete at least two elective credits. Students enrolled in the forty-five-day classes should be enrolled in classes that will give them elective credits; for example, where you see Power English is where additional writing, reading, and comprehension competencies are stressed. Most states' education departments have courses with labels that can become these electives.

When reviewing schedules such as figure 6.10, some educators oppose the plan because students are not enrolled in other core classes such as science and social studies; however, little is gained by enrolling students in classes where there is a high probability of failure. This model, when implemented with fidelity, will offer students the chance to earn six to eight credits toward graduation in most states. Plus they will build competencies that should increase their success in future core classes.

VERSION I				
Period	**Semester 1**		**Semester 2**	
	Forty-five days	Forty-five days	Forty-five days	Forty-five days
1	Reading or literacy-related course	Power English	Power algebra	Algebra I
2				
3				
4				
Lunch	Thirty minutes			
I/E	Forty minutes			
5	Mathematics fundamentals		English 9	
6				
7	Physical education		Technology	
8				
VERSION II				
Period	**Semester 1**		**Semester 2**	
	Forty-five days	Forty-five days	Forty-five days	Forty-five days
1	Mathematics fundamentals	Power algebra	Power English	English 9
2				
3				
4				
Lunch	Thirty minutes			
I/E	Forty minutes			
5	Reading or literacy-related course		Algebra I	
6				
7	Day 1: Physical education		Day 1: Physical education	
8	Day 2: Technology		Day 2: Technology	

*I/E is intervention and enrichment.

Figure 6.10: Examples of forty-five-day intensive schedules for grade 9 students.

For many students, the alternative has been to spend their first year in high school failing several courses, earning few credits, and not building any competencies that will help them in future courses. See chapters 4–7 in *Block Scheduling* (Canady & Rettig, 1995) for additional scheduling variations.

Similar to figure 6.10, figure 6.11 illustrates a thirty-day intensive schedule. Some schools might call this their *rescue schedule* because this format works for students who are reaching the minimum age to legally drop out of school and still have earned a limited number of core credits (ten Carnegie Units or less). By the age of sixteen or seventeen, these students often are repeating two or three mathematics or English courses and credit recovery programs, which typically do not produce college- or career-ready graduates (Gewertz, 2016a). These under-credited and overage students are likely never to get a high school diploma if they are continually placed in six to eight classes that run year-long in single periods (Rath, Rock, & Laferriere, 2012). These students often lack organizational skills and motivation. They also may have little or no support outside of the school day. They need to have short-term goals established for them and to receive school support in reaching those goals.

VERSION I					
	Semester 1			Semester 2	
				Potential Re-entry to Modified Four-by-Four Semester Schedule	
	Thirty Days	Thirty Days	Thirty Days		
Block I	Core one	Core two	Core three	Core one	
Block II	Core one	Core two	Core three	Core two	
Intervention and enrichment period					
Lunch					
Block III	Elective one or core			Elective two or core three	
Block IV	Core one	Core two	Core three	Core three or four	

VERSION II						
	Semester 1			Semester 2		
	Thirty Days	Thirty Days	Thirty Days	Thirty Days	Thirty Days	Thirty Days
Block I	Core one	Core two	Core three	Core four	Core five	Core six
Block II	Core one	Core two	Core three	Core four	Core five	Core six
Intervention and enrichment period						
Lunch						
Block III	Elective one			Elective two		
Block IV	Core one	Core two	Core three	Core four	Core five	Core six

Figure 6.11: Modified four-by-four semester high school thirty-school-day block schedule for students needing intensive acceleration and support.

High schools that follow such a schedule include a core class for credit and then an elective class such as physical education, technology, or music for sixty to ninety minutes. That kind of class is required in most schools so that the core teachers working with a single-class group can schedule their planning periods. With this schedule, struggling students do not spend as much time attending courses they are likely to fail as they do in traditional schedules. In addition, the thirty-day schedule enables teachers to focus on fewer students at a time and to address the specific needs of individuals within those smaller groups. Clearly, teachers are more likely to provide additional support to students in a single class of twenty students than when they are carrying 120-plus students in courses that run all year.

Figure 6.12 (page 94) shows two plans, A and B, which can be modified to reduce the failing time for selected students. Plan A is designed for students who have failed because of excessive absences or who need to master only a few concepts—not the major concepts of the course—and need little or no teacher support. Plan B is designed for students who need additional instruction with support from the teacher providing the initial instruction. Once the seat time requirement has been met in the failing class, instruction can be focused on mastery of basic core standards; for example, when such students can pass the end-of-course assessment for the class, as the CCSS outline, then they can receive credit. In the repeat class, students should not simply repeat the content the same way it was presented during the first semester. Rather, teachers should assess student learning to determine what concepts they have not mastered. For some students, the focus of the repeat course may need to be on a limited number of standards, which then would be considered a trailer course that they can complete in a shorter time. Then, both the repeat class and instructional support can be focused on those standards. A quality software program can help with scheduling this differentiated instruction. In addition, for grades 9 and 10, this schedule works for any middle school experiencing a large number of student failures at the close of semester one.

The preceding schedules illustrate how traditional high schools can provide support for various student cohorts. Alternative high schools may also adopt schedules to provide support for the particular types of students they serve. In the following section, we provide examples of schoolwide schedules at three different alternative schools.

VERSION A		
Period	**Semester 1**	**Semester 2**
One	Course one (Eighty minutes)	Repeat or trailer course one (Fifty minutes)
Two		Individual support, re-teaching, reassessing, or new course for some students (Sixty minutes)
Three	Course two (Eighty minutes)	
Four		Repeat or trailer course two (Fifty minutes)
Lunch	(Thirty minutes)	(Thirty minutes)
I/E	(Forty minutes)	(Forty minutes)
Five	Course three (Eighty minutes)	New course (Eighty minutes)
Six		
Seven	Course four (Eighty minutes)	New course (Eighty minutes)
Eight		
VERSION B		
Period	**Semester 1**	**Semester 2**
One	Course one (Ninety minutes)	Repeat or trailer course one (Forty-five minutes)
Two		Support for repeat course one
Three	Course two (Ninety minutes)	Repeat or trailer course two (Forty-five minutes)
Four		Support for repeat course two
Lunch	(Thirty minutes)	(Thirty minutes)
I/E	(Forty minutes)	(Forty minutes)
Five	Course three (Ninety minutes)	New course (Ninety minutes)
Six		
Seven	Course four (Ninety minutes)	New course (Ninety minutes)
Eight		

*I/E is intervention and enrichment.

Source: Adapted from Rettig & Canady, 2000.

Figure 6.12: Scheduling adaptations designed to accommodate first-semester failing students using four-by-four semester schedule for grades 7 through 10.

Alternative School Schedules

All educators encounter students who are low performing, discouraged, possibly lacking the family support necessary to concentrate on their schoolwork, and likely to drop out of school or leave school undereducated. For such students—who also may lack personal motivation and organizational skills—classes that run for a full

180-day school year can be especially daunting. For many of these students, it is helpful to focus on one core subject at a time, as the following example of Fork Union Military Academy in Fork Union, Virginia, shows. Some of these students may also need short-term learning goals, strict attendance requirements, and high behavior standards, as illustrated by the Daylight/Twilight Alternative High School in Trenton, New Jersey. Other students may benefit from innovative scheduling combined with instructive community and business relationships, as Pathways in Technology Early College High School (P-TECH) in New York City offers.

In addition to the schedule adaptations, the following three case studies of alternative scheduling reveal additional options for using time effectively. Schedules are a basic aspect of schooling, and it's important to consider how educators can adjust schedules to provide more effective instruction and reduce failing time for students.

Fork Union Military Academy

Since 1950, an unusual scheduling plan—the one-subject plan—has been in effect at the upper school at Fork Union Military Academy (www.forkunion.com), a boarding school. Fork Union adopted a scheduling variation to meet the needs of students experiencing academic difficulties, and the results are impressive.

In grades 9 through 12, the academic year is divided into five grading periods of about seven weeks each—that's not unusual. What *is* unusual is that each student is assigned to *one* core course during each grading period. With five grading periods, students accumulate a total of five core course credits in each school year. Classes meet every day, Monday through Friday, and sometimes on Saturday for additional classroom time. Class size is never more than twenty students. Each teacher instructs only one group of students during each grading period.

Emphasizing one subject at a time immerses students in that particular subject, not scattering their attention among a typical high school load of several subjects. Teachers get to know their students very well; they are able to use a wide variety of instructional methods and make individualized assignments according to needs. They can check student work daily and provide detailed feedback to each student about that work. And teachers find much flexibility in day-to-day scheduling, such as arranging field trips as needed and holding class in the library when the students need to conduct research for their term papers.

Fork Union Military Academy (n.d.) saw its honor roll double in size within the first five years of implementing the one-subject plan, even though it uses a grading scale of A is 95 percent and F is 75 percent and below. Over the ensuing years, this improvement has persisted and is now matched by improvements in preliminary SAT (PSAT) and SAT scores. To date, even though not all graduates apply immediately to colleges, Fork Union Military Academy (n.d.) graduates' college acceptance rate is 100 percent.

Daylight/Twilight Alternative High School

Daylight/Twilight Alternative High School (www.trenton.k12.nj.us/daylight twilightalternativehigh_home.aspx), a public high school in New Jersey, is another that has a schedule that meets students' needs by focusing on one core class at a time. Daylight/Twilight serves students in grades 9 through 12 who have faced varied challenges in traditional schools. In the Daylight 30/60 day course program, "students take one four-hour course each day, for thirty days, then receive five [New Jersey] credits. Simultaneously, students also enroll in a two-hour elective course, for sixty days of school, and upon completion receive five [New Jersey] credits" (Daylight/ Twilight High School, n.d.). Students take these courses in three eighty-minute blocks daily. In New Jersey, five credits is equal to one Carnegie Unit (hours of class time with an instructor). The 30/60 instructional cycle provides students with increased daily class time, increased focused on course skills, and increased ability to earn high school credits (Daylight/Twilight High School, n.d.). Additionally, students are able to focus on one course at a time and set and meet short-term goals. Daylight/Twilight school also has a twilight program that operates three days a week from 4 to 8 p.m. and serves students ages twenty-one and older (PolicyOptions, n.d.). In addition, the Daylight/Twilight school offers a credit-recovery program that gives students the opportunity to make up failed courses through online instruction (Daylight/Twilight High School, n.d.).

Traditional schools can provide various types of schedules, some of which are illustrated in this chapter, within the framework of one bell schedule. For this type of scheduling to succeed, the scheduling team needs to design data-driven schedules that serve student needs. For example, a traditional high school can establish a learning center in the three core subject areas—English, mathematics, and science—that students most often fail (Gewertz, 2016a). In each learning center, courses can be organized on a thirty-day schedule where students repeat courses they have failed or complete trailer courses.

Pathways in Technology Early College High School

Pathways in Technology Early College High School (P-TECH; www.ptechnyc .org), a collaboration of the New York City Department of Education, the New York

College of Technology, and the IBM Corporation, exemplifies alternative scheduling that promotes student success. P-TECH creates college and industry partnerships with the goal of 100 percent of students earning a high school diploma and an associate degree within six years. The school offers enrichment sessions four evenings a week, plus four evening sessions per week that offer credit-bearing courses.

Principal Rashid Davis (2012) outlines the major scheduling strategies leading to the success of P-TECH:

- P-TECH has a ten-period day that includes five required teaching periods, plus an optional sixth teaching period and periods for course preparation, professional development, and lunch.

- Some teachers offer (and are paid for) an additional sixth teaching period. This extra teaching period enables P-TECH students to receive 21 percent more instructional time than most high school students.

In addition to scheduling, Davis (2012) cites staffing and the strategic use of data and monitoring as the keys to the school's success. Much like the standards-based grading approach, Davis (2012) recognizes that students may require multiple attempts to reach proficiency or college-readiness targets. Thus, P-TECH monitors students' progress, and staff members seek to instill resiliency in students.

Summary

The various elementary, middle, and high school schedules in this chapter give teachers structured time to support struggling students. Combined with standards-based grading, this reimagining of the school day (and school year) provides the basic ingredients needed to boost student achievement and increase the number of college- and career-ready graduates.

Visit **go.SolutionTree.com/instruction** for more example schedules including three separate high school cohorts.

Reflection Questions

Use the following questions to help initiate faculty discussions and to assist faculty in examining the potential of revised scheduling.

1. How does class period length become a factor in determining whether the school day is fragmented for both teachers and students?

2. Do expectations of students change as students change teachers and spaces? If so, what are the consequences for students?

3. How chaotic are transitions at your school or district? Are valuable instructional minutes being squandered?

4. How can you adopt or adapt the practices of the case studies described in this chapter? How could each of the schedules illustrated benefit students in your school?

5. What support do you need from school administrators to revise your school's schedule? How can you obtain that support?

EPILOGUE

The Power of a Teacher

Most of us can identify a teacher who had exceptional abilities to inspire, motivate, teach, excite and, in some instances, change the direction of our lives. Hopefully, we had very few, if any, who gave us scar tissue. Robert Lynn Canady had the good fortune of having a speech teacher named Miss Dockie, who possessed all the attributes typically used to describe exceptional teachers. She also followed many of the recommended instructional and grading practices described in this text. In the more than sixty-five years that have passed since he was Miss Dockie's student, Robert often has thought how many lives could be positively changed if all students could have at least one Miss Dockie during their school years. Here he describes his experience.

▲ ▲ ▲ ▲ ▲

In high school, I was blessed to have a teacher who built her classroom control by emphasizing positive characteristics in students. She seemed to see something good in every student, and students tried to live up to her expectations. We never wanted to disappoint Miss Dockie, as most of her students called her. I am certain I would not have even gone to college if I had not had this teacher. She made it very difficult for students to fail, but she also made it very difficult to get good grades, praise, and rewards without doing work and rework. She made us redo assignments (for example, a speech or preparation for a debate) until she determined that our work met her standards. She also gave us very focused feedback. She would explain to us what we needed to do to meet the standards.

In Miss Dockie's classes, we could take risks. We knew she was not looking for ways to fail us, and she did not throw roadblocks in our way. She was not an easy teacher; we felt secure in her classroom, and we wanted to perform well for her and for ourselves. I could name many incidents where she offered encouragement and hope! She was honest with students. There was no false praise; she always stressed that if we worked and stayed with the task, she would be there to help us. She made us feel we could succeed. I have come to believe that students must know they will be rewarded for work and for rework—not just for their initial high grades. Students have control over their work habits; they have little control over their family structures or their basic intellectual capacity, be it large or small.

When I was a junior or senior in high school, a group of us participated in a forensics tournament in Nashville, Tennessee. In those days a school won a trophy on the basis of total points the entire school team earned, but we had to have students compete in all the elements of the tournament. As I recall, we had to have a debate team, and we had to have a person perform in poetry interpretation, one in extemporaneous speaking, one in humorous and dramatic declamations, and so on. Our school was very competitive in these tournaments, and we took great pride in winning them. I can recall going up the steps of one of Nashville's large high schools and hearing students from other schools say: "Oh, no! Dickson High School is here. We have to compete against them!" Of course, those comments made us all want to do well, but keep in mind that to win we had to individually do well and earn points.

The incident I am going to relate happened over sixty-five years ago, but I remember it vividly. Usually, I did well in those tournaments, but that night I had to be the one to do extemporaneous speaking, which was the speaking assignment the majority of students disliked the most. In that element of the tournament, I had to draw a topic out of a box. For about ten minutes I had to review a current periodical, such as *Time* magazine, and plan a presentation. Certain procedures had to be followed when we presented. That night I did not do well and was ranked low. I personally could accept my low ranking, except that it was my performance that kept the school from winning the trophy that evening.

When the other students in my group learned about my performance causing the loss, they began teasing me. In the 21st century, we likely would call it bullying. Of course their comments hurt; I already felt bad enough. When we got into the car to return home, two of the students continued making negative comments to me, and I remember the exact words Miss Dockie said very emphatically: "We shall have none of that talk! What we shall focus on tonight is: what did we *all* learn from this experience?" Then she explained that two other students (she did not name them) had requested that they not do the element of the tournament that I had accepted, and she further explained how we had to have participants in all elements of the contest even to be considered for the trophy. She went on to say that she had studied the comment sheets from the judges and that two of the rules we were expected to follow had not been well publicized and that in the next tournament (four weeks later) each student in the car would be prepared to compete in extemporaneous speaking.

Looking back, I think it was amazing how she was able to take the heat off me and involve the students in a lively discussion on how we all could become better. In the next tournament, I did the same element of speaking, although privately Miss Dockie told me that she considered insisting another student do the extemporaneous speaking element, but she thought I would feel better if I could redeem myself. She also said she would help me improve my skills with extemporaneous speaking—and she did. In the next tournament, I got high rankings, and the school won the trophy. What would have happened if Miss Dockie had taken a different approach with the other students and me the night my low performance lost the trophy?

Some people would say that I have become an international workshop presenter (forty-six states, the Virgin Islands, and Dependent Schools in Germany); yet, I have many limitations as a speaker. During the summer after my senior year (1949–1950), I decided I wanted to become a radio announcer; this was before the days of television in most homes. I feel sure Miss Dockie had doubts about my becoming a radio personality, but she never told me I should not consider such a calling. Instead, she arranged for me to have an interview and a tryout at one of the Nashville radio stations, now the home station of The Grand Ole Opry. Of course, with my deep regional accent and difficulty pronouncing and enunciating certain words, I did not do well at the radio tryout. The radio station officials were kind, but they did burst my balloon!

Following that experience, Miss Dockie explained to me what she saw as my strengths and challenges if I wanted to continue in a vocation that required speaking to large audiences. Although this occurred more than six decades ago, I still remember what she said. First, she explained what the people at the radio station had told me, and she said that she agreed with them. Again, I wish to point out that this teacher was honest with students; she did not give false hope or praise. Some of what she said to me I did not fully understand at the time, but now I think I do. She agreed that I had some rather serious speech deficits (I think she called them *warts*)—referring to my Southern accent, hillbilly drawl, mispronunciation of certain words, and the like—but she told me that I had three strengths and that, if I built on them, she thought I could be a successful speaker.

The three strengths she told me I possessed (I still remember them!) were as follows: (1) you have a great sense of timing and can tell a story in an interesting way; (2) you have a sense of humor and can laugh at yourself; and (3) you are authentic so people will believe you. She went on to say that if I would develop these three strengths, most people would overlook my speaking flaws. Although I have not intentionally tried to focus on the feedback she gave me, I believe her observations were correct in explaining my limited success as a speaker. Maybe a goal of *great* teachers is to help students come to believe they can do the work, but sometimes students need help and encouragement. Some students also must learn how to overcome their deficits and how to build on their strengths.

I remain very appreciative of Miss Dockie believing in and supporting me at a critical time in my young life. During the first year of my teaching, I recall visiting her and expressing my appreciation for what she had done for me. I still remember her response: "Oh, Lynn, if I have helped you, then you must do the same for others; that way my success lives on." Although not as effective as Miss Dockie, I hope I have at least partially fulfilled her legacy.

Possibly the last time I talked with Miss Dockie was after I married and lived in Chattanooga. My wife and I were visiting my parents in Dickson during the Christmas holidays, and my mother told me she had heard that Miss Dockie retired. I decided to drop by. In those days, in small towns and rural areas of the South, people did not have to call first if they wanted to visit someone. Soon after I knocked on Miss Dockie's Poplar Street door, she opened the door widely and exclaimed: "Oh, Lynn, you are the seventh student who has come to see me during the holidays!" Then she added: "You know, Lynn, the Bible says 'If you cast your bread upon the waters, it will come back to you,' but mine has come back as cake!"

In this day of educational accountability and the stress on test scores, I still often think of Miss Dockie and how great teachers and great school leaders are so very important to society. (In my opinion, great school leaders also are great teachers, possibly in a different way!) Great teachers do far more than improve test scores. In addition to developing their students' competencies, great teachers expand their visions, which can have a positive influence not only in the lives of individuals and families but ultimately in society, that continues for generations.

I have read about the importance of developing resiliency, *grit*, in students. Educators seem to agree on the value of programs that focus on developing resiliency. These programs help students learn how to bounce back from failure. They help rebuild resiliency by not distorting their own reality and by identifying and building on their strengths. Angela Lee Duckworth, in her discussion, includes these characteristics but adds: "So grit is not just having resilience in the face of failure, but also having deep commitments that you remain loyal to over many years" (as cited in Perkins-Gough, 2013).

I doubt if Miss Dockie would have used terms like *resilience* and *grit* in describing how she treated students, but I have reflected over multiple experiences I had with her. She taught her students, probably unknowingly, not to be overcome with failure, but to analyze correctly and plan a way to grow from such experiences; that when the hurdles were too challenging, take corrective action and move on. She helped students, with her support, grow from failure. She was honest with students, and she provided focused feedback and support. She seemed to know when to push and when to pull back.

It might sound strange, but I do not think this teacher had the word *no* in her thinking or in her vocabulary. I recall several instances when she was told she could not do something with or for her students, and she acted as if she had not heard the rejection. Such a response seemed to motivate her to find another way to move her students forward. I also saw her model this philosophy in her personal life.

I still can hear Miss Dockie making statements such as "The third point in your argument is not logical; tell me why and tell me how you can fix it." If I could not answer her question successfully, she typically would mediate the question to see if I could come up with a solution, or sometimes she would ask other students how they would fix the problem. In another instance, she might state: "The beginning of your speech does not grab your audience. How could you change the opening?" or, "You lose the reader after the first two pages; consider moving your major point on page 4 to page 3 and reworking the paper."

Of course, bigger issues that Miss Dockie addressed still linger in my thoughts: "Think about what you do well; focus on your strengths. Let's find another way to reach your goal. You might have to work harder than some students, but you can succeed." For more than sixty-five years I have been reminded of those words and have found them helpful. Miss Dockie had a passion for her teaching, and with that passion she conveyed to her students that she cared and that she was there to support us in our stumbling, incremental patterns of growth. My goal is that all youngsters find a Miss Dockie in their lives. Thank you, Miss Dockie.

Reflection Questions

Use the following questions to help initiate faculty discussions and assist faculty to examine the potential of becoming exceptional educators.

1. Describe the characteristics of two teachers who had a significant impact on your life in a positive way. What lessons have you practiced with your own students because of those teachers?

2. Describe the characteristics of two teachers who had a significant impact on your life in a negative way. What lessons have you practiced with your own students because of those teachers?

3. How do you wish to be remembered as an educator?

References and Resources

Achieve. (2013, March). *Students with disabilities and the Common Core State Standards resources*. Accessed at www.achieve.org/files/CCSS-SWDs-Resources-Mar2013.pdf on February 10, 2016.

Allen, R. (2011). How to increase student engagement and achievement with peer tutors. *Education Update, 53*(4), 1–4.

Allensworth, E. M., & Easton, J. Q. (2007). What matters for staying on-track and graduating in Chicago public high schools: A close look at course grades, failures, and attendance in the freshman year (Research Report). Chicago: Consortium on School Research. Accessed at https://consortium.uchicago.edu/sites/default/files/publications/07%20What%20Matters%20Final.pdf on February 11, 2016.

Allensworth, E. M., & Easton, J. Q. (2008). *Early warning systems that support students at risk of dropping out of high school* (Research Brief). Washington, DC: Center for Comprehensive School Reform and Improvement. Accessed at http://files.eric.ed.gov/fulltext/ED504129.pdf on November 21, 2016.

Allington, R. L. (2011). What at-risk readers need. *Educational Leadership, 68*(6), 40–45.

Annie E. Casey Foundation. (2010). *Early warning! Why reading by the end of third grade matters—A KIDS COUNT special report from the Annie E. Casey Foundation.* Accessed at www.aecf.org/m/resourcedoc/AECF-Early_Warning_Full_Report-2010 .pdf on November 21, 2016.

Astone, N. M., & McLanahan, S. S. (1994). Family structure, residential mobility, and school dropout: A research note. *Demography, 31*(4), 575–584.

Balfanz, R., & Byrnes, V. (2012). *The importance of being in school: A report on absenteeism in the nation's public schools*. Baltimore: Center for Social Organization of Schools.

Biddle, B. J., & Berliner, D. C. (2002). Small class size and its effects. *Educational Leadership, 59*(5), 12–23.

Canady, C. E. (2013, January). Grading policies at J.F. Burns Elementary School, Kings Local School District, Kings Mills, Ohio. *J.F. Burns Elementary School News.*

Canady, C. E., & Canady, R. L. (2012). Catching readers up before they fail. *Educational Leadership, 69*. Accessed at www.ascd.org/publications/educational-leadership/jun12 /vol69/num09/Catching-Readers-Up-Before-They-Fail.aspx on February 10, 2016.

Canady, R. L. (n.d.a). *Comparing an educational system which is organized primarily to* sort and select *with a standards-driven system which is structured to* teach and learn. Accessed at www.robertlynncanady.com/canady/comparingsystems.pdf on November 21, 2016.

Canady, R. L. (n.d.b). *Grading practices that increase/decrease the odds for student success: General grading information packet.* Accessed at www.robertlynncanady .com/canady/grading/Grading-Packet-10–11.pdf on March 20, 2016.

Canady, R. L. (n.d.c). *School practices/policies that may contribute to school failure for selected students.* Accessed at www.robertlynncanady.com/canady/SchoolPractices.pdf on February 6, 2017.

Canady, R. L. (1988). A cure for fragmented schedules in elementary schools. *Educational Leadership, 46*(2), 65–67.

Canady, R. L., & Hotchkiss, P. R. (1989). It's a good score! Just a bad grade. *Phi Delta Kappan, 71*(1), 68–71.

Canady, R. L., & Rettig, M. D. (1995). *Block scheduling: A catalyst for change in high schools.* Larchmont, NY: Eye on Education.

Canady, R. L., & Rettig, M. D. (2008). *Elementary school scheduling: Enhancing instruction for student achievement.* Larchmont, NY: Eye on Education.

Carnegie Foundation for the Advancement of Teaching. (2014). *50-state scan of course credit policies* (Working draft). Accessed at www.carnegiefoundation.org/wp-content /uploads/2013/08/CUP_Policy_MayUpdate1.pdf on September 1, 2016.

Carnegie Unit and Student Hour. (n.d.). In *Wikipedia*. Accessed at http://en.wikipedia .org/wiki/Carnegie_Unit_and_Student_Hour on February 10, 2016.

Cavanagh, S. (2012, March 5). States loosening 'seat time' requirements. *Education Week*. Accessed at www.edweek.org/ew/articles/2012/03/07/23biz-state.h31.html on February 10, 2016.

Center for Public Education. (2012). *Credit recovery programs: Full report.* Accessed at www.centerforpubliceducation.org/Main-Menu/Staffingstudents/Credit-recovery -programs/Credit-recovery-programs-full-report.html on October 17, 2016.

Center for Research on Teaching and Learning. (n.d.). *Study skills*. Accessed at www.crlt .umich.edu/tstrategies/tsss on September 17, 2016.

Chang, H. (2010, September 10). Five myths about school attendance. *Education Week*. Accessed at www.edweek.org/ew/articles/2010/09/15/03chang.h30.html on February 11, 2016.

Chang, H. N., & Romero, M. (2008). *Present, engaged, and accounted for: The critical importance of addressing chronic absence in the early grades.* New York: National Center for Children in Poverty. Accessed at www.nccp.org/publications/pub_837.html on February 10, 2016.

Chiles, N. (2013, July). Saving our sons: The miseducation of black boys. *Ebony,* 122–127.

Collins, K., Connors, K., Davis, S., Donohue, A., Gardner, S., Goldblatt, E., et al. (2010). *Understanding the impact of trauma and urban poverty on family systems: Risks, resilience, and interventions.* Los Angeles, CA: National Child Traumatic Stress Network. Accessed at www.nctsnet.org/sites/default/files/assets/pdfs/understanding _the_impact_of_trauma.pdf on November 21, 2016.

Common Core State Standards Initiative. (n.d.a). *Frequently asked questions.* Accessed at www.corestandards.org/about-the-standards/frequently-asked-questions on November 1, 2014.

Common Core State Standards Initiative. (n.d.b). *Development process.* Accessed at www .corestandards.org/about-the-standards/development-process on November 1, 2014.

Cooper, H. (2001). *The battle over homework: Common ground for administrators, teachers, and parents.* Thousand Oaks, CA: Corwin Press.

Cooper, H. (2006, September 23). Does homework improve academic achievement? [Editorial]. *Duke Today.* Accessed at https://today.duke.edu/2006/09/homework _oped.html on February 10, 2016.

Cooper, H., Robinson, J. C., & Patall, E. A. (2006). Does homework improve academic achievement? A synthesis of research, 1987–2003. *Review of Educational Research, 76*(1), 1–62.

Davis, R. F. (2012). P-TECH: Where we are now. *Citizen IBM.* Accessed at www.ibm .com/blogs/citizen-ibm/2012/10/p-tech-where-we-are-now.html on October 18, 2012.

Dawson, P. (n.d.). *Homework: A guide for parents.* Bethesda, MD: National Association of School Psychologists. Accessed at www.nasponline.org/Documents/Resources %20and%20Publications/Handouts/Families%20and%20Educators/Homework _a_Guide_for_Parents.pdf on February 10, 2016.

Daylight/Twilight High School. (n.d.). *Daylight/Twilight High School.* Accessed at http://files.campus.edublogs.org/daylightblogs.org/dist/7/206/files/2012/06 /BrochureDTHS_INSIDE_pic-1ugouuz.jpg on February 3, 2017.

Deaton, A. (2013). *The great escape: Health, wealth, and the origins of inequality.* Princeton, NJ: Princeton University Press.

Donen, T., Anton, J., Beard, L., Stinson, T., & Sullivan, G. (2010). *Grades don't matter: Using assessment to measure true learning.* Nashville, TN: Armour & Armour. Accessed at www.gradesdontmatter.org on July 15, 2016.

DuFour, R. (2004). What is a professional learning community? *Educational Leadership, 61*(8), 6–11.

Dweck, C. S. (2014, November). *The power of believing that you can improve* [Video file]. Accessed at www.ted.com/talks/carol_dweck_the_power_of_believing_that_you_can_improve on February 10, 2016.

Dynamic Learning Maps. (n.d.). *Overview.* Accessed at http://dynamiclearningmaps .org/#sthash.UDFzqM2L.dpuf on February 10, 2016.

Fagan, M. (2011, September 6). Letter grades giving way to 'standards-based' marks in Lawrence schools. *Lawrence Journal-World.* Accessed at www2.ljworld.com/news/2011 /sep/06/letter-grades-giving-way-standards-based-marks-law on February 10, 2016.

Farbman, D. A., Goldberg, D. J., & Miller, T. D. (2014). *Redesigning and expanding school time to support Common Core implementation.* Washington, DC: Center for American Progress. Accessed at www.americanprogress.org/wp-content/uploads /2014/01/CommonCore6.pdf on December 4, 2016.

Ferguson, N. (2011, October 23). Yes, Wall Street helps the poor. *Newsweek.* Accessed at www.newsweek.com/yes-wall-street-helps-poor-68189 on February 11, 2016.

Finn, J. D., & Achilles, C. M. (1990). Answers and questions about class size: A statewide experiment. *American Educational Research Journal, 27*(3), 557–577.

Fisher, D., & Frey, N. (2007). Implementing a schoolwide literacy framework: Improving achievement in an urban elementary school. *The Reading Teacher, 61*(32–45). Accessed at www.hsigarland.org/ReadingRoost/resources/research%20articles /implementing%20a%20schoolwide%20litearcy%20framework.pdf on November 21, 2016.

Fisher, D., & Frey, N. (2008). Releasing responsibility. *Educational Leadership, 66*(3), 32–37.

Fork Union Military Academy. (n.d.). *The one subject plan.* Fork Union, VA: Author. Accessed at www.forkunion.com/uploaded/Download_Forms_Center/One_Subject _Plan/onesubjectplan.pdf on February 10, 2016.

Gewertz, C. (2016a, April 13). High school coursework seen falling short. *Education Week.* Accessed at www.edweek.org/ew/articles/2016/04/13/only-8-percent-of-grads -take-enough.html on August 22, 2016.

Gewertz, C. (2016b, November 16). With 95 kinds of high school diplomas, what does 'graduation' mean? High school coursework seen falling short. *Education Week.* Accessed at http://blogs.edweek.org/edweek/high_school_and_beyond/2016/11 /what_does_a_high_school_diploma_mean.html on November 21, 2016.

Goodwin, B. (2011). Research says / grade inflation: Killing with kindness? *Effective Grading Practices, 69*(3), 80–81.

Gould, E. D., Weinberg, B. A., & Mustard, D. B. (2002). Crime rates and local labor market opportunities in the United States: 1979–1997. *Review of Economics and Statistics, 84*(1), 45–61. Accessed at www.mitpressjournals.org/doi/abs/10.1162 /003465302317331919#.V8bVFfkrLrd on August 31, 2016.

Great Schools Partnership. (2014). *The glossary of education reform.* Accessed at http:// edglossary.org on July 15, 2016.

Greenberg, E., Dunleavy, E., & Kutner, M. (2007). *Literacy behind bars: Results from the 2003 National Assessment of Adult Literacy Prison Survey* (NCES 2007–473). Washington, DC: National Center for Education Statistics.

Grossman, T., Reyna, R., & Shipton, S. (2011). *Realizing the potential: How governors can lead effective implementation of the Common Core State Standards.* Washington, DC: National Governors Association. Accessed at www.nga.org/files/live/sites/NGA/files /pdf/1110CCSSIIMPLEMENTATIONGUIDE.PDF on February 11, 2016.

Guskey, T. R. (1996). Reporting on student learning: Lessons from the past—Prescriptions for the future. In T. R. Guskey (Ed.), *Communicating student learning: 1996 yearbook of the Association for Supervision and Curriculum Development* (pp. 13–24). Alexandria, VA: Association for Supervision and Curriculum Development.

Guskey, T. R. (2006). Making high school grades meaningful. *Phi Delta Kappan, 87*(9), 670–675.

Guskey, T. R. (2011). Five obstacles to grading reform. *Educational Leadership, 69*(3), 16–21. Accessed at www.ascd.org/publications/educational-leadership/nov11/vol69 /num03/Five-Obstacles-to-Grading-Reform.aspx on February 11, 2016.

Guskey, T. R. (2013). The case against percentage grades. *Educational Leadership, 71*(1), 68–72.

Guskey, T. R. (2015). *On your mark: Challenging the conventions of grading and reporting.* Bloomington, IN: Solution Tree Press.

Guskey, T. R., & Jung, L. A. (2006). The challenges of standards-based grading. *Leadership Compass, 4*(2), 6–10.

Hart, B., & Risley, T. R. (1995). *Meaningful differences in the everyday experience of young American children.* Baltimore: Brookes.

Hawkins, J. D., Catalano, R. F., & Miller, J. Y. (1992). Risk and protective factors for alcohol and other drug problems in adolescence and early adulthood: Implications for substance abuse prevention. *Psychological Bulletin, 112*(1), 64–105.

Haycock, K. (2001). Closing the achievement gap. *Educational Leadership, 58*(6), 6–11.

Henderson, N. (2013). Havens of resilience. *Educational Leadership, 71*(1), 22–27. Accessed at www.ascd.org/publications/educational-leadership/sept13/vol71/num01 /Havens-of-Resilience.aspx on February 11, 2016.

Heppen, J. B., & Therriault, S. B. (2008, July). *Developing early warning systems to identify potential high school dropouts* (Issue brief). Washington, DC: National High School Center.

Hill, D. (2014). *Brick house: How to defeat student apathy by building a brick house culture.* Lebanon, TN: JJ & Zak.

Hill, D., & Nave, J. (2009). *Power of ICU: The end of student apathy . . . reviving engagement and responsibility.* Maryville, TN: Southland Books.

Hull, J. (2011). *Starting out right: Pre-K and kindergarten—Full report*. Alexandria, VA: Center for Public Education. Accessed at www.centerforpubliceducation.org/Main -Menu/Organizing-a-school/Starting-Out-Right-Pre-K-and-Kindergarten/Starting -Out-Right-Pre-K-and-Kindergarten-full-report.html on February 11, 2016.

The Huffington Post. (2008, July 11). *Standards-based grading slow to take effect in high schools*. Accessed at www.huffingtonpost.com/2012/07/11/standards-based-grading -s_n_1665377.html on December 4, 2016.

Ihrke, D. K., & Faber, C. S. (2012, December). *Geographical mobility: 2005 to 2010— population characteristics*. Washington, DC: U.S. Census Bureau. Accessed at www .census.gov/prod/2012pubs/p20–567.pdf on February 11, 2016.

Indiana University. (2012, November 15). *IU study: Homework doesn't improve course grades but could boost standardized test scores* [Press release]. Accessed at http:// newsinfo.iu.edu/news/page/print/23471.html on February 10, 2016.

Jung, L. A., & Guskey, T. R. (2010). Grading exceptional learners. *Educational Leadership*, *67*(5), 31–35.

Karoly, L. A., & Bigelow, J. H. (2005). *The economics of investing in universal preschool education in California* [Executive summary]. Santa Monica, CA: RAND Corporation. Accessed at www.rand.org/pubs/monographs/MG349z1.html on February 10, 2016.

Keefe, J. W., & Jenkins, J. M. (2002). Personalized instruction. *Phi Delta Kappan*, *83*(6), 440–448.

Kindler, A. L. (1995). Education of migrant children in the United States. *Directions in Language and Education*, *1*(8).

Kohn, A. (2006). *The homework myth: Why our kids get too much of a bad thing*. Cambridge, MA: Da Capo Press.

Kohn, A. (2007). Rethinking homework. *Principal*, *86*(3), 35–38.

Koumpilova, M. (2013, March 28). Minnesota schools give standards-based grading system a closer look. *Twin Cities Pioneer Press*. Accessed at www.twincities.com /2013/03/28/minnesota-schools-give-standards-based-grading-system-a-closer-look -2 on February 10, 2016.

Lacour, M., & Tissington, L. D. (2011). The effects of poverty on academic achievement. *Educational Research and Reviews*, *6*(7), 522–527. Accessed at www.academicjournals .org/journal/ERR/article-full-text-pdf/31F3BFB6129 on September 2, 2016.

Lassahn, N. E. (n.d.) *History of grading systems*. Accessed at www.ehow.com/about _5103640_history-grading-systems.html on April 19, 2016.

Lenz, B., & Kay, K. (2013). Two paths: How will you see the Common Core? *Edutopia*. Accessed at www.edutopia.org/blog/common-core-two-paths-bob-lenz-ken -kay on November 13, 2016.

Lezotte, L. W. (2008). *Effective schools: Past, present, and future*. Accessed at www .effectiveschools.com/images/stories/brockpaper.pdf on February 10, 2016.

Levy, E. (2007). *Gradual release of responsibility: I do, we do, you do.* Accessed at www
.sjboces.org/doc/Gifted/GradualReleaseResponsibilityJan08.pdf on February 6, 2017.

Maltese, A. V., Tai, R. H., & Fan, X. (2012). When is homework worth the time?
Evaluating the association between homework and achievement in high school
science and math. *The High School Journal, 96*(1), 52–72.

Morsy, L., & Rothstein, R. (2015). Five social disadvantages that depress student
performance: Why schools alone can't close achievement gaps. *Economic Policy
Institute.* Accessed at www.epi.org/publication/five-social-disadvantages-that
-depress-student-performance-why-schools-alone-cant-close-achievement-gaps on
November 4, 2016.

National Center and State Collaborative. (2012). *About the NCSC.* Accessed at http://
ncscpartners.org/about-states on February 10, 2016.

National Center for Education Statistics. (2008). *Table 381. Labor force participation rates
and employment to population ratios of persons 16 to 64 years old, by highest level of
education, age, sex, and race/ethnicity: 2007.* Accessed at https://nces.ed.gov/programs
/digest/d08/tables/dt08_381.asp on February 10, 2016.

National Center for Education Statistics. (2015a). *The Nation's Report Card: 2015
mathematics and reading assessments—National results overview for reading.*
Accessed at www.nationsreportcard.gov/reading_math_2015/#reading?grade=4
on December 4, 2016.

National Center for Education Statistics. (2015b). *The Nation's Report Card: 2015
mathematics and reading assessments.* Accessed at www.nationsreportcard.gov/reading
_math_2015/#?grade=4 on December 4, 2016.

National Center for Education Statistics. (2016). *Family characteristics of school-
age children.* Accessed at http://nces.ed.gov/programs/coe/indicator_cce.asp on
December 4, 2016.

National Governors Association Center for Best Practices. (2012). *State strategies for
awarding credit to support student learning* (Issue Brief). Washington, DC: Author.
Accessed at www.nga.org/files/live/sites/NGA/files/pdf/1202EDUCREDIT
BRIEF.PDF on December 4, 2016.

National Governors Association Center for Best Practices, Council of Chief State School
Officers, & Achieve. (2008). *Benchmarking for success: Ensuring U.S. students receive a
world-class education.* Accessed at www.achieve.org/files/BenchmarkingforSuccess.pdf
on December 4, 2016.

Neild, R. C., & Balfanz, R. (2006). An extreme degree of difficulty: The educational
demographics of the urban neighborhood high school. *Journal of Education for
Students Placed at Risk, 11*(2), 123–141.

O'Connor, K. (2011). *A repair kit for grading: 15 fixes for broken grades* (2nd ed.). Boston:
Pearson.

O'Connor, K., & Wormeli, R. (2011). Reporting student learning. *Educational Leadership,
69*(3), 40–44.

Ouchi, W. G. (2009). *The secret of TSL: The revolutionary discovery that raises school performance.* New York: Simon & Schuster.

Penno, J. F., Wilkinson, I. A., & Moore, D. W. (2002). Vocabulary acquisition from teacher explanation and repeated listening to stories: Do they overcome the Matthew effect? *Journal of Educational Psychology, 94*(1), 23.

Perkins-Gough, D. (2013). The significance of grit: A conversation with Angela Lee Duckworth. *Educational Leadership, 71*(1), 14–20. Accessed at www.ascd.org /publications/educational-leadership/sept13/vol71/num01/The-Significance-of-Grit@ -A-Conversation-with-Angela-Lee-Duckworth.aspx on September 19, 2016.

PolicyOptions.org. (n.d.). *Daylight/Twilight school.* Accessed at www.policyoptions.org /trenton/organization/daylighttwilight-school on February 10, 2016.

Portwood, S. G., Ayers, P. M., Kinnison, K. E., Waris, R. G., & Wise, D. L. (2005). YouthFriends: Outcomes from a school-based mentoring program. *Journal of Primary Prevention, 26*(2), 129–188.

Power of ICU. (n.d.). *Mabank Junior High School.* Accessed at www.poweroficu.com /spotlights/MabankJH.pdf on February 10, 2016.

Putnam, R. D. (2015). *Our kids: The American dream in crisis.* New York: Simon & Schuster.

Rath, B., Rock, K., & Laferriere, A. (2012). *Helping over-age, under-credited youth succeed: Making the case for innovative education strategies.* Accessed at www.opp.org /docs/Helping%20Over-Age%20Under-Credited%20Youth%20Succeed%20 -%20OPP,%20July%202012.pdf on December 4, 2016.

Reeves, D. B. (2004). The case against the zero. *Phi Delta Kappan, 86*(4), 324–325. Accessed at http://missionliteracy.com/uploads/3/1/5/8/3158234/caseagainstzero.pdf on December 4, 2016.

Reeves, D. B. (2008). Leading to change: Effective grading. *Educational Leadership, 65*(5), 85–87. Accessed at www.ascd.org/publications/educational-leadership/feb08/vol65 /num05/Effective-Grading-Practices.aspx on December 4, 2016.

Resmovits, J. (2012, May 17). Education report: Chronic absenteeism undermines over 5 million students. *The Huffington Post.* Accessed at www.huffingtonpost.com/2012 /05/17/absent-students-chronic-absenteeism-dropouts_n_1522673.html on February 10, 2016.

Rettig, M. D. & Canady, R. L. (1998, March). High failure rates in required mathematics courses: Can a modified block schedule be part of the cure? *NASSP Bulletin, 82*(596), p. 56–65.

Rettig, M. D., & Canady, R. L. (2000). *Scheduling strategies for middle schools.* Larchmont, NY: Eye on Education.

Rich, M. (2014, July 20). Obama to report widening of initiative for black and Latino boys: My Brother's Keeper program grows to include more impoverished minorities. *The New York Times.* Accessed at www.nytimes.com/2014/07/21/education/obamas -my-brothers-keeper-education-program-expands.html on July 21, 2014.

Rothstein, R. (2014, January 7). The urban poor shall inherit poverty. *The American Prospect.* Accessed at http://prospect.org/article/urban-poor-shall-inherit-poverty on September 3, 2016.

Scherer, M. (2011). Perspectives / What we learn from grades. *Educational Leadership, 69*(3), 7–9. Accessed at www.ascd.org/publications/educational-leadership/nov11 /vol69/num03/What-We-Learn-from-Grades.aspx on December 4, 2016.

Schimmer, T. (2016). *Grading from the inside out: Bringing accuracy to student assessment through a standards-based mindset.* Bloomington, IN: Solution Tree Press.

Schmidt, P. (2007). High school students aim higher without learning more, federal studies find. *Chronicle of Higher Education, 53*(27), A32.

Scriffiny, P. L. (2008). Seven reasons for standards-based grading. *Educational Leadership, 66*(2), 70–74.

Simons-Morton, B. G., Crump, A. D., Haynie, D. L., & Saylor, K. E. (1999). Student– school bonding and adolescent problem behavior. *Health Education Research, 14*(1), 99–107.

Skyward. (n.d.). *The standards-based backlash: A transition guide for superintendents* [White paper]. Accessed at www.skyward.com/Discover/White-Papers/The-Standards-Based -Backlash on February 3, 2017.

Sparks, S. D. (2013, September 10). "Growth mindset" gaining traction as school improvement strategy. *Education Week.* Accessed at www.edweek.org/ew/articles /2013/09/11/03mindset_ep.h33.html on February 10, 2016.

Stanovich, K. E. (1986). Matthew effects in reading: Some consequences of individual differences in the acquisition of literacy. *Reading Research Quarterly, 21*(4), 360–407.

Stiggins, R. J. (2004). New assessment beliefs for a new school mission. *Phi Delta Kappan, 86*(1), 22–27.

Stiggins, R. J. (2007). Assessment through the student's eyes. *Educational Leadership, 64*(8), 22–26.

Suskind, D., Suskind, B., & LeWinter-Suskind, L. (2015). *Thirty million words: Building a child's brain—Tune in, talk more, take turns.* New York: Dutton.

Tomlinson, C. A., & McTighe, J. (2005). What really matters in teaching? (The students). *ASCD Express.* Accessed at www.ascd.org/ascd-express/vol1/105-tomlinson-mctighe .aspx on February 9, 2016.

Topping, K. (2008). *Peer-assisted learning: A practical guide for teachers.* Newton, MA: Brookline Books.

Trenton Public Schools. (n.d.). *Daylight Twilight Alternative High School: About us.* Accessed at www.trenton.k12.nj.us/aboutus1496.aspx on February 10, 2016.

Twenge, J. M., & Campbell, W. K. (2008). Increases in self-views among high school students: Birth cohort changes in anticipated performance, self-satisfaction, self- liking, and self-competence. *Psychological Science, 19*(11), 1082–1086.

U.S. Department of Labor, Bureau of Labor Statistics. (2014). *How the government measures unemployment.* Accessed at www.bls.gov/cps/cps_htgm.pdf on November 4, 2016.

U.S. Department of Labor, Bureau of Labor Statistics. (2015a). *Employment projections: Earnings and unemployment rates by educational attainment, 2015.* Accessed at www.bls.gov/emp/ep_chart_001.htm on February 10, 2016.

U.S. Department of Labor, Bureau of Labor Statistics. (2015b). *Employment projections: Occupations that need more education for entry are projected to grow faster.* Accessed at www.bls.gov/emp/ep_table_education_summary.htm on February 10, 2016.

U.S. Department of Labor, Bureau of Labor Statistics. (2016). *Earnings and unemployment rates by educational attainment: Earnings and unemployment rates by educational attainment, 2015.* Accessed at www.bls.gov/emp/ep_table_001.htm on August 31, 2016.

Van Horn, M. L., Jaki, T., Masyn, K., Ramey, S. L., Smith, J. A., & Antaramian, S. (2009). Assessing differential effects: Applying regression mixture models to identify variations in the influence of family resources on academic achievement. *Developmental Psychology, 45*(5), 1298–1313. doi:10.1037/a0016427

Vance, J. D. (2016). *Hillbilly elegy: A memoir of a family and culture in crisis.* London: HarperCollins UK.

Vatterott, C. (2009). *Rethinking homework: Best practices that support diverse needs.* Alexandria, VA: Association for Supervision and Curriculum Development.

Vatterott, C. (2010). Five hallmarks of good homework. *Educational Leadership, 68*(1), 10–15.

Vatterott, C. (2015). *Rethinking grading: Meaningful assessment for standards-based learning.* Alexandria, VA: Association for Supervision and Curriculum Development.

Walpole, S., & McKenna, M. C. (2013). *The literacy coach's handbook: A guide to research-based practice* (2nd ed.). New York: Guilford Press.

Walpole, S., & McKenna, M. C. (2016). *Organizing the early literacy classroom: How to plan for success and reach your goals.* New York: Guilford Press.

Weaver, C. (2002). *Reading process and practice* (3rd ed.). Portsmouth, NH: Heinemann.

Werner, E. (2003). Foreword. In N. Henderson & M. M. Milstein, *Resiliency in schools: Making it happen for students and educators* (pp. vii–ix). Thousand Oaks, CA: Corwin Press.

The White House, Office of the Press Secretary. (2014, May 30). *Opportunity for all: My brother's keeper blueprint for action* (Fact Sheet and Report). Accessed at www.whitehouse.gov/the-press-office/2014/05/30/fact-sheet-report-opportunity-all-my-brother-s-keeper-blueprint-action on February 10, 2016.

Wiggins, G. (2012). Seven keys to effective feedback. *Educational Leadership, 70*(1), 10–16. Accessed at www.ascd.org/publications/educational-leadership/sept12/vol70/num01/Seven-Keys-to-Effective-Feedback.aspx on September 13, 2016.

WiseGeek. (n.d.). *What is the history of the K–12 education system?* Accessed at www .wisegeek.com/what-is-the-history-of-the-K-12-education-system on February 10, 2016.

Wolin, S. J., & Wolin, S. (1993). *The resilient self: How survivors of troubled families rise above adversity.* New York: Villard Books.

Wood, J. (2013, July 1). *Common Core State Standards—What's the controversy?* Portland, OR: Northwest Evaluation Association. Accessed at www.nwea.org/blog/2013 /common-core-state-standards-whats-the-controversy on December 4, 2016.

Woodruff, D. J., & Ziomek, R. L. (2004). *High school grade inflation from 1991 to 2003* (Research Report Series 2004–04). Iowa City, IA: ACT.

Wormeli, R. (2006). *Fair isn't always equal: Assessing and grading in the differentiated classroom.* Portland, ME: Stenhouse.

Wormeli, R. (2011). Redos and retakes done right. *Educational Leadership, 69*(3), 22–26.

Wren, S. (2000). *The cognitive foundations of learning to read: A framework.* Austin, TX: Southwest Educational Development Laboratory.

Wright, R. G. (1994). Success for all: The median is the key. *Phi Delta Kappan, 75*(9), 723–725.

Index

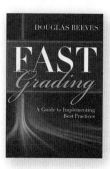

FAST Grading
Douglas Reeves
Embrace effective grading procedures that have the power to reduce failure rates and encourage learning. Discover practical strategies teachers and administrators can use to ensure their grading practices center on four essential criteria: fairness, accuracy, specificity, and timeliness.
BKF647

Building a Common Core–Based Curriculum
Susan Udelhofen
Explore various stages of curriculum development, from the preliminary work of building academic support to creating curriculum maps and tracking improvement goals. Learn to effectively share information during the curriculum-building process, and engage in significant, collaborative conversations around the curriculum.
BKF549

Elements of Grading
Douglas Reeves
The author provides educators with practical suggestions for making the grading process more fair, accurate, specific, and timely. In addition to examples and case studies, new content addresses how the Common Core State Standards and new technologies impact grading practices.
BKF648

It's About TIME
Edited by Austin Buffum and Mike Mattos
Carve out effective intervention and extension time at all three tiers of the RTI pyramid. Explore more than a dozen examples of creative and flexible scheduling, and gain access to tools you can use immediately to overcome implementation challenges.
BKF609, BKF610